DYNAMIC
DAMES

50 Leading Ladies Who Made History

•••••◆•••••

SLOAN DE FOREST

RUNNING PRESS

PHILADELPHIA

Running Press
Hachette Book Group
1290 Avenue of the Americas,
New York, NY 10104
www.runningpress.com
@Running_Press

Printed in China

First Edition: July 2019

Published by Running Press, an imprint of Perseus Books, LLC, a subsidiary of Hachette Book Group, Inc. The Running Press name and logo is a trademark of the Hachette Book Group.

The Hachette Speakers Bureau provides a wide range of authors for speaking events. To find out more, go to www.hachette speakersbureau.com or call (866) 376-6591.

The publisher is not responsible for websites (or their content) that are not owned by the publisher.

Page ii: Dorothy Dandridge on the set of *Carmen Jones*.
Page iii: A wardrobe test for Elizabeth Taylor in *Cleopatra*.
Print book cover and interior design by Amanda Richmond.

Library of Congress Control Number: 2019931465

ISBNs: 978-0-7624-6552-1 (hardcover), 978-0-7624-6550-7 (ebook)

1010

10 9 8 7 6 5 4 3 2 1

HAIR DRESSING DEPT.
PROD. # J-03

ELIZABETH TAYLOR "CLEOPATRA"
Wig #6   Sc. # 339
Chg + 44
Set. Int. Throne
Rm. 16 - 8X10

Contents

BIG BAD MAMAS

FATAL FEMMES

LADIES WHO LAUGH

WOMEN OF MYSTERY

STRONG SURVIVORS

SUPERHEROINES

Foreword

My heroes have all been female. Maybe women were more
accessible. They were teachers. Hazel Wright—Sunday school. Carmelita Maracci—dance.
Terry Cole-Whittaker—life.

Women in the movies were my teachers, too. To me, Rita Hayworth had everything. She danced, spoke, and moved beautifully. I studied Spanish dancing with her father and her uncle, the Cansinos. Columbia Pictures chief Harry Cohn—bully, hustler, notorious in his time—masterminded her career. With his studio behind her, he brought her to the masses. But it was Rita who held the cards. Power seeks beauty. Look at the millions of people who travel across the world to see the Taj Mahal, built in tribute to a beloved wife, Mumtaz. It was she who inspired her emperor.

Sex, no matter how you write about it, is the real currency. On the screen, it's behind the words. Mae West crafted every bon mot she voiced around it. Marlene Dietrich conquered at least two continents and millions of men with it. But true screen goddesses are possessed with more than beauty and sex appeal. While it may have been whispered that Bette Davis was less than beautiful, it made no difference. She used her eyes to force your attention. Her physical carriage star-lighted any space she inhabited. When

Joan Crawford walked into a room, the weather changed. She even commanded that the temperature of her sets be eight to ten degrees colder than the rest of the studio.

Katharine Hepburn exhorted dignity in a space with anyone. The only actor substantial enough for her talents was Spencer Tracy. In *Adam's Rib*, their male-female one-upmanship was carefully crafted by the best writers in the business. In the *Thin Man* movies, there was the hilarious hijinks of William Powell's four-drink gumshoe up against Myrna Loy's calm brilliance. I love Maureen O'Hara's passionate yet levelheaded Irishness. She was John Wayne's true equal. But I would have to nominate Olivia de Havilland as the most successful dynamic dame of all. Living beyond 100 years takes more than genes. Character and integrity, anyone?

As Catwoman on the *Batman* TV series, I played a very different type of dynamic dame: scheming, sensuous, short-suffering; the fantasy female of diabolical plots. In those days, women superheroes (or supervillains) were virtually nonexistent.

Julie Newmar as Catwoman

Catwoman was in a class by herself. Maybe that's why ladies still approach me to tell me how that confident, cat-suited bad girl inspired and empowered them.

Today, we have Gal Gadot as Wonder Woman, Emma Watson as Hermione Granger, Halle Berry as Storm, and super-powered girls galore. Yet the audience has become the real celebrity. That's what they go to the movies for—to be transported, to become the superheroes and superheroines they didn't know they already are.

Whether playing out fantasies is our full-time job or not, I believe everyone gets to place their foot in the cement of history. It's only recently that empowerment has been the primary force for female attention. The world changes. Something's coming, something that's wanted or needed. In the pages of this book, you'll see that it's been building for a long time. You will relive cinematic history through the incredible women profiled in *Dynamic Dames*, a compendium of feminine force that is at once entertaining, informative, and inspirational.

—Julie Newmar

Introduction

What makes the dames in this book so dynamic?

Not their looks—though they certainly are easy on the eyes—nor their charismatic person-alities, killer wardrobes, or crackling dialogue. Dynamic dames share an X-factor: they tran-scend the narrow confines of their gender role, whether by taking small steps or revolution-ary strides. Each of these fifty women, in her unique way, is an architect of her own destiny. By taking charge of their lives, by refusing to be marginalized, these characters motivate us with their resilience, delight us with their high spirits, and thrill us with their audacity.

Our look at extraordinary screen sirens begins in the Jazz Age with the feisty Clara Bow, an untrained actress who redefined the feminine ideal and became, as F. Scott Fitzgerald observed, "the quintes-sence of what the term 'flapper' signifies." Nearly a century after Clara caused a stir as hyper-flirtatious Alverna in *Mantrap* (1926), strong, sexy Gal Gadot embodied the modern superheroine archetype in *Won-der Woman* (2017), stopping bullets in their tracks and lassoing evildoers into submis-sion. In the years between, a vast array of fascinating femmes have earned their place in these pages. Outspoken powerhouses like Bette Davis in *Ex-Lady* (1933) and Julia Roberts as *Erin Brockovich* (2001) mix and mingle with Melanie Griffith's soft-spoken secretary Tess in *Working Girl* (1988) and Whoopi Goldberg's long-suffering Celie in *The Color Purple* (1985). Celluloid icons such as Vivien Leigh in her immortal

characterization of Scarlett O'Hara and Joan Crawford's unforgettable Mildred Pierce are celebrated here, but so too are lesser-known ladies, like the effervescent Josephine Baker as *Zouzou* (1934) and groundbreaking B-movie babe Pam Grier as *Coffy* (1973). Some are as familiar as old friends, others may be surprising new dis-coveries, but all are women who reach just a little bit farther than expected to claim their strength and power.

Selecting only fifty of the most empow-ered heroines in film history is a daunting task when there are thousands of heroic, inspiring ladies to choose from. What about those who didn't make the cut? Among others are Anna May Wong rising from dishwasher to dancing sensation in *Picca-dilly* (1929); spunky Ginger Rogers cracking an egg over a lecherous stranger's head in *The Major and the Minor* (1944); Olivia de Havilland transforming from naïve maiden

Pam Grier in *Coffy*

Vivien Leigh in *Gone with the Wind*

to woman of steel in *The Heiress* (1949); Diane Keaton marching to her own drummer in *Annie Hall* (1977); six-year-old Quvenzhané Wallis steering her own life journey in *Beasts of the Southern Wild* (2012); and Emma Stone clobbering her male-chauvinist opponent as tennis champ Billie Jean King in *Battle of the Sexes* (2017). The list could go on and on. It is my hope that this book will function as a gateway to exploring these and more aspirational female characters, though not as a definitive list of the greatest women in cinema. That would require several volumes!

The fact is, powerful women have been a part of the movies from the very begin-

ning, both on camera and behind the lens. One of the first filmmakers in history was a woman: France's Alice Guy Blaché, who began directing in 1896. During and after World War I, Mary Pickford was not only the world's most popular movie star, but also one of Hollywood's wealthiest moguls as the head of her own production company and the cofounder of United Artists. Pickford's partner in crime was Frances Marion, the industry's top scenarist in the 1920s and early 1930s and the first screenwriter to win two Oscars.

On the screen, fictional females dominated the classic era of motion pictures. Indeed, the 1930s and early 1940s were a

Gal Gadot in *Wonder Woman*

Golden Age of sorts for women. In 1935, producer Samuel Goldwyn estimated that 70 percent of movie audiences were female. Half of the major stars were female, too (Joan Crawford, Bette Davis, Barbara Stanwyck, Greta Garbo, and Mae West led the pack of powerful leading ladies), and over one-third of Hollywood films were written, cowritten, or based on stories written by women. A few, such as Dorothy Arzner (and, a little later, Ida Lupino), directed as well. After World War II, a gradual shift occurred. Movies with women in the lead role dwindled, and by the early 1970s, Hollywood's target audience was mostly male, as were the top box-office stars.

Mae West in *I'm No Angel*

Right now, as I write this book, the motion-picture industry is on the cusp of a sea change. The pendulum has started to swing toward a healthier balance of power between male and female filmmakers, between strong leading men and equally strong leading ladies. It won't happen overnight. But we can be inspired to move forward by looking back at the amazing characters in this book, brought to vibrant life by amazing women—the actresses who played them, and, in many cases, female writers, producers, and directors, too.

As actress and gender-equity advocate Geena Davis once observed, "Identifying with a character is one of the best parts of seeing a movie, but as women, we've had to train ourselves to experience the male journey." Here's to all the beautiful, assertive, entertaining, and dynamic dames who have served as tour guides for the female journey. Just as important, here's to all the dynamic female characters yet to be created.

—Sloan De Forest,
September 30, 2018

Pre-Code Bad Girls

The Motion Picture Production Code of 1934 was a form of self-censorship that constricted the movies until it started to crumble in the liberal climate of the 1960s. Under the Code, nudity and profanity were forbidden, and sinful behavior never went unpunished. But before the Code was strictly enforced in July of 1934, women in the talkies could get away with murder. A career? Check. Premarital sex? Sure. Extra-marital affairs? Bring 'em on. Almost nothing was taboo for these liberated ladies. And the actresses who brought them to life were often just as thrilling off the screen as on.

Clara Bow
AS "ALVERNA"

Mantrap (1926)

In 1932, Clara Bow caused a stir in the risqué cult classic
Call Her Savage, her pre-Code comeback about a scandalous Texas heiress who resorts to prostitution, among other eyebrow-raising exploits. But Bow had risen to stardom in silent films. In the Roaring Twenties, before the movies learned to talk, she had pulled herself out of the Brooklyn slums to become the patron saint of uninhibited young flappers everywhere. Of the fifty-plus films she made before retiring from Hollywood at age twenty-eight, her personal favorite was Victor Fleming's 1926 comedy *Mantrap.* When you watch the movie, it's easy to see why. Though not technically pre-Code, this late-era silent gives Bow a starring role that predicts the dynamic ladies of the pre-Code era.

From the moment she steps on the scene as Alverna, a bubbly, spit-curled Kewpie doll of a manicurist with a severe flirting addiction, Clara "just walks away with the picture," to quote *Variety.* "Every minute she's in it," the critic wrote, "she steals it." For some reason, the lovely Alverna falls for the ungainly Joe (Ernest Torrence), a simple backwoodsman who makes her his bride and snatches her away to his cabin in the rustic Canadian town of Mantrap. Take Alverna's boredom and flirting problem, add in Ralph (Percy Marmont), a New York divorce lawyer running away from loose city women, and you have more than a love triangle; you have two fellas caught in the ultimate mantrap.

Aided by master cinematographer James Wong Howe and screenwriters Adelaide Heilbron and Ethel Doherty (adapting the novel by Sinclair Lewis), Clara Bow really shines. Heilbron and Doherty took significant liberties with Lewis's story, making Alverna more likable and heroic. The role encapsulates everything the public loved about Clara: Alverna was good-hearted, fun-loving, and just a little bit naughty. Back when screen women were sharply divided into two categories—virgin or vamp—Clara managed to carve out her own distinctive niche right in the middle.

In the scene where she feeds Joe and Ralph chocolates and bops around to a jazz record, Clara displays her trademark manic

Clara Bow as Alverna in *Mantrap*

Ernest Torrence, Percy Marmont, Clara Bow, Victor Fleming, and James Wong Howe on the set

energy. According to Paramount chief Adolph Zukor, "She danced even when her feet were not moving. Some part of her was in motion in all her waking moments—if only her great rolling eyes." Clara was animator Max Fleischer's inspiration for Betty Boop, and, in *Mantrap*, her resemblance to the famous cartoon character is remarkable. But there's a tough, independent streak beneath the adorable exterior. When Joe and Ralph join forces against her on a camping trip, Alverna tells them off, hijacks their only boat, and ditches them both. Joe shouts after her, "Remember, you still bear my name," to which she retorts, "So does your old man!" Giggling, she sails off into the sunset, leaving the two men stranded in the wilderness. This is Alverna's big moment—funny, sassy, and triumphant. At the end of the picture, she returns to Joe, but it's clear that he will

have to accept her as she is. Flirting, for her, is as natural as breathing.

"May I interrupt your funny act just long enough to say that I'm my own boss— from now on?"

—"ALVERNA"

The success of *Mantrap* led Clara to her most iconic role in *It* (1927), the movie that would make her known everywhere as "The It Girl." She was on top of the world—until sound replaced silents. Early sound technology often required actors to stand still and speak into hidden microphones (see *Singin' in the Rain* [1952] for a comical take on the talkie revolution), which deflated the magical spontaneity of stars like Clara Bow. Her career took a nosedive, and she left the movies at age twenty-five.

But Clara had the final word. She returned to the screen in grand style when Fox offered her a quarter-million-dollar deal that included creative control of her films. She starred in *Call Her Savage* and the carnival romance *Hoopla* (1933), her celluloid swan song. After that, she retired, had children with her husband (cowboy star Rex Bell), and quietly became a legend—an unforgettable symbol of everything that was fun and untamed about the Jazz Age.

Did You Know?

Clara Bow wanted her Alverna to be as naughty as the adulterous character in the Sinclair Lewis novel. She once told a reporter, "She was bad in the book, but—darn it!—of course, they couldn't make her that way in the picture. So I played her as a flirt."

Clara Bow and Percy Marmont on location near San Bernardino, California

Norma Shearer

AS "JERRY MARTIN"

The Divorcée (1930)

Think Sharon Stone caused a sensation by uncrossing her legs in *Basic Instinct* (1992)? That's nothing compared to the furor Norma Shearer unleashed when she played a wife who has an affair with her husband's best friend in *The Divorcée*. A woman cheating on her husband was nothing new, even in 1930. What made Shearer's Jerry Martin different was the absolution of sin. This was no dime-store floozy. This was an educated, virtuous lady who convinced the audience that her adultery was perfectly justified. As a woman hell-bent on sexual equality with men, Shearer lit a fuse that set Hollywood on fire and incinerated any lingering traces of Victorian oppression. She shocked the movie-going public, ignited the pre-Code sexual revolution, and even altered society's definition of "*that* kind of woman."

Jerry is an ultra-modern female who wears slinky gowns without underwear and warns her fiancé, Ted (Chester Morris), that she won't wait long to marry him because she's "human." Ted compliments Jerry on her "man's point of view" and agrees to an equal marriage. That is, until he cheats on her and she "balances their accounts" by sleeping with Ted's pal, the eternally inebriated but gorgeous Don (Robert Montgomery). When Ted finds out, suddenly he's not so cool with equality; the union ends in divorce, and Jerry embarks on an international spree of romantic liaisons with attractive males across the globe. Its star made headlines for her daring depiction of a lady liberated by divorce.

"Norma Shearer has crusaded for women," reporter Gladys Hall declared in a 1932 article in *Motion Picture* magazine. By starring in *The Divorcée* and its equally provocative follow-up, *A Free Soul* (1931), Shearer, Hall wrote, "has killed our grandmothers. I mean, she has killed what they stood for. . . . She has cremated the myth that men will never marry 'that kind of woman.'" What Hall was saying is that, in a time when "good" women were expected to be virgins, Shearer made it acceptable for women to have premarital sex and affairs, just as men do. She evened the playing field.

Norma Shearer with the Academy Award she received for *The Divorcée*

Stricken with remorse (or maybe just exhausted from her many amorous escapades), Jerry reunites with Ted at the close of the picture. But she's not begging for forgiveness because she has done wrong; instead, she's realized that a dozen men can't replace the one she truly loves. So it's a win-win for Jerry: she gets even with Ted's fling, leaves him to enjoy the company of who-knows-how-many lovers, then is allowed to return to her beloved ex-husband in the end. She has an extraordinary amount of personal freedom, rarely matched on the screen since.

Ex-Wife, the source novel for *The Divorcée*, was so scandalous that it was initially published anonymously. Its author, Ursula Parrott (born Katherine Ursula Towle), is sadly forgotten today, though she penned four screenplays, fifty short stories, and twenty-two novels. Boasting friends and colleagues like F. Scott Fitzgerald, Sinclair Lewis, and Zane Grey, with whom she collaborated on *The Woman Accused* (1933), Parrott lived as large as one of her heroines, marrying four different men and raking in royalties from her popular fiction yarns.

Shearer, too, is unjustly overlooked these days, despite her enormous fame in the 1930s. Ever ambitious, Edith Norma Shearer scrapped her way to stardom in silent pictures, overcoming a lazy right eye, a slightly pudgy figure, and a disastrous first screen test the actress herself described as "hideous." But Norma had a few aces up her sleeve: luminous alabaster

Norma Shearer and Chester Morris

The famous George Hurrell photograph that won Shearer the role

Robert Montgomery, Norma Shearer, and Chester Morris in *The Divorcée*

> "I'm glad I discovered there's more than one man in the world while I'm young and they want me....From now on, you're the only man in the world that my door is closed to!"
> —"JERRY MARTIN"

skin, a mane of bobbed brunette waves that could be boyishly sleek when pushed behind her ears or wild when tousled and tumbling over one eye, and a smooth, cultured speaking voice that helped propel her to the big leagues when sound came along. Her 1927 marriage to MGM's production manager Irving Thalberg didn't hurt either.

Thalberg purchased the rights to *Ex-Wife* with plans to cast Joan Crawford in the lead, doubtful that his wife was sexy enough to pull it off. Waging a no-holds-barred campaign for the role, Norma sat for a seductive portrait with glamour photographer George Hurrell to prove she

had the right stuff. She not only nabbed the to-die-for part, but also took home the Academy Award for Best Actress, inspiring the industry to follow her example and produce a wave of earthy movies about boundary-pushing broads. You go, Norma.

Did You Know?

When Nick Grindé, John Meehan, and Zelda Sears adapted Parrott's novel for the screen, they changed the heroine's name from Patricia to Jerry, a more masculine-sounding moniker. This served as a cue to the audience that this woman was on equal footing with men.

Bette Davis

AS "HELEN BAUER"

Ex-Lady (1933)

"I don't want to be like my mother, the yes-woman for some man. I want to be a person of my own," declares modern young career gal Helen to her fiancé, Don, played by the hunky blond Gene Raymond. Though Don begs—and though her parents are outraged at their living arrangement—she refuses to marry him, preferring instead to live together in an equal partnership. She just knows that the instant they make it legal she'll be demoted from lover to subservient spouse. She'll be expected to give up her job as an in-demand magazine illustrator to stay at home and take care of Don. In short, he will have the right to tell her what to do. "No one," she warns Don, "has any rights about me except me."

Ex-Lady was a racy pre-Code gem from Warner Bros. that gave the incomparable Bette Davis her first top-billed role. While the title suggests that Bette has a tarnished reputation, the movie takes her side. No accusations, no judgments. Her character is allowed to be as bad as she wants to be. And, as ads for *Beyond the Forest* (1949) would assert years later, "Nobody's as good as Bette when she's bad." Davis would cement her image as a force to be reckoned with as she matured. By the time she costarred with Joan Crawford in *What Ever Happened to Baby Jane?* (1962) at age fifty-four, Bette was a legend in her own time. Her reported feud with Crawford was legendary as well and would later be fictionalized in the 2017 miniseries *Feud: Bette and Joan.*

Even in her early days, Bette earned a reputation as a bold babe with no fear of speaking her mind or bucking the system. Ruth Elizabeth Davis was on the cusp of twenty-five when she starred as Helen Bauer, and was three years away from her first Best Actress Academy Award, for *Dangerous* in 1936. That was the same year she played hooky from Warner Bros., first breaching her contract, then accusing the studio of "slavery" by forcing her into "mediocre pictures." Bette lost the court case, but she won Warners' eventual respect and meatier roles. In 1939, she would score a second Oscar for donning a scandal-

Bette Davis as Helen Bauer in *Ex-Lady*

ously sexy red dress as the town trollop in *Jezebel.*

With smart, stylish direction by B-movie maestro Robert Florey, *Ex-Lady* is a highly polished remake of the 1931 film *Illicit,* starring Barbara Stanwyck. Both movies were based on a 1930 play by Edith Fitzgerald and her then boyfriend Robert Riskin, an unmarried couple writing a taboo-shattering comparison of wedded versus unwedded bliss.

———◇———

"When I'm forty, I'll think of babies. In the meantime, there are twenty years in which I want to be the baby, play with my toys, and have a good time playing with them…. I don't want to be a wife!"

—"HELEN BAUER"

———◇———

Marriage, Helen says, would make her boring before her time. "It's dull!" she wails. As embodied by a lissome, platinum-blonde Bette in gowns by Orry-Kelly, Helen is an elegantly dressed firecracker. She wants to be with Don exclusively, but they argue over the double standards applied to women in marriage. Finally, Helen turns the tables and proposes to Don. Following a sultry Havana honeymoon, just as she predicted, the couple settles into a dull routine; before long, they grow restless. Don and Helen both indulge in short-lived affairs with others. But after a trial separation, they realize they're better together than apart. The union of marriage "may not be perfect," Helen admits, "but this way it hurts less."

In the end, she agrees to remain Don's wife, but it's *her* choice. She commits to the arrangement because they love each other and want to be together, and the only socially acceptable way to accomplish that is with wedding rings. But being a Mrs. doesn't define her; she gets to keep her career and her man. And her headstrong personality suggests that she'll never be completely tamed. Helen Bauer, like Bette Davis, was a forward-thinking lady in a movie decades ahead of its time.

Did You Know?

Ex-Lady was a little too sensationalistic for Bette Davis. She later called the film "a piece of junk" and "an ecstasy of poor taste."

Top: Gene Raymond, Bette Davis, and Robert Florey. Bottom: Bette Davis and Monroe Owsley

Barbara Stanwyck
AS "LILY POWERS"

Baby Face (1933)

Though she took up less space in the gossip columns, Barbara Stanwyck did just as much to define twentieth-century American womanhood as her contemporaries Joan Crawford and Bette Davis. Over the course of a career spanning nearly sixty years, Babs played women who were very good, women who were very bad, and every shade of gray in between—and she played the hell out of them. In her pre-Code days, she embodied the Depression-hardened dame, the kind of broad who was just as likely to slug a guy in the jaw as kiss him.

One of Stanwyck's most remarkable roles is in *Baby Face,* a movie so outrageously risqué that it was censored even in 1933, when the atmosphere was as loose as the ladies on the screen. Censors and critics alike lambasted the film for its "gaudiness" and, as the *Los Angeles Times* complained in 1933, for just plain showing "too much sexiness." As Lily Powers, Stanwyck is openly sexual, self-centered, greedy, and ambitious—all cardinal sins for women in this era—but manages to keep the audience on her side. Though uneducated, she exudes enough confidence and street smarts to rule the world. Her very name is symbolic of the modern woman: Lily, a beautiful flower on the outside, and Powers, a surprising strength underneath.

Stanwyck had a hand in shaping the character, collaborating on the story concept with producer Darryl Zanuck. Kathryn Scola, who cowrote the script with Gene Markey, was a prolific female screenwriter who specialized in controversial themes. Typical of the gritty, fast-paced movies Warner Bros. was known for back in the dirty thirties, *Baby Face* wastes no time getting to the point. Young Lily starts out in Pittsburgh, slinging gin and fending off men in her father's grimy speakeasy, and literally sleeps her way up to a swanky Manhattan penthouse by the third reel. When the camera pans up the exterior of the bank where she works, we know she is ascending the professional ranks one bed at a time.

But she doesn't do it alone. She is guided

Barbara Stanwyck as Lily Powers in *Baby Face*

"Know what's in this bag? Half a million dollars.
Someday I'll have the other half that goes with it."
—"LILY POWERS"

by her Nietzsche-reading guru, Mr. Cragg (Alphonse Ethier), who convinces Lily to turn the tables on the opposite sex. "You must use men," he advises her, "not let them use you. You must be a master, not a slave.... Use men to get the things you want!" Her accomplice in this pursuit is her sidekick, Chico (Theresa Harris), a black woman whom she employs as a maid but treats as an equal and a friend—an uncommon relationship for the time period. Harris, a beautiful triple-threat talent who rarely got the chance to play anything besides domestics, sparkles in one of her juiciest roles. Seeing Harris in *Baby Face* inspired Lynn Nottage to write the 2011 play *By the Way, Meet Vera Stark*, a comedy about an African American maid who becomes a stage star.

Using Cragg's strategy, Lily makes out like gangbusters. Every single man she seduces (including a strapping young John Wayne) becomes a slave to her charms. Whether engaged, happily married, or upstanding paragons of virtue, the boys fall

DYNAMIC DAMES

Barbara Stanwyck and Theresa Harris

for her like a row of dominoes. They make it so easy. Lily, however, does not rely on sex alone; she works at self-improvement, sharpening her grammar, her job skills, and her fashion sense as she grows her bank account. Chico transforms into an elegant, glamorous lady right alongside her gal pal.

Naturally, it's too good to last. Lily finally meets her match in the new bank president, wealthy Courtland Trenholm (George Brent). Though she ends up turning over all her riches to him when he meets a financial crisis, this wasn't enough for the Hays Office (as many referred to the film censorship board). They demanded several edits and a new ending in which Lily not only relinquishes her ill-gotten fortune, but is also banished to the outskirts of Pittsburgh from whence she came. In the censored version, Mr. Cragg's advice to enslave men becomes a warning not to take "the wrong way." This places the blame squarely on Lily's shoulders, and she becomes little more than a naughty woman who breaks the rules and must be punished.

Lily may have lost in the end, but Barbara Stanwyck's star power only increased. In 1944, she embodied a character that made Lily Powers look like a saint: Phyllis Dietrichson in Billy Wilder's quintessential film noir *Double Indemnity*. As one of cinema's most unforgettable femme fatales, Stanwyck as Dietrichson "calls the shots" and "generally raises the bar for

Barbara Stanwyck in a publicity portrait for *Baby Face*

female badness," noted film professor Sheri Chinen Biesen. She also earned her third of four Oscar nominations. Hollywood eventually wised up, presenting Stanwyck with an honorary Academy Award in 1982.

Did You Know?

The significantly edited Hays Office-approved cut of *Baby Face* was the only version the world had seen until 2004, when the original cut was discovered and screened.

Mae West

AS "TIRA"

I'm No Angel (1933)

When dynamic dame Madonna decided to shock and titillate the public in 1992, she released a book titled *Sex*. Though it certainly got people talking, the concept was nothing new; Mae West had already worked that angle sixty-six years earlier when she had written and starred in the 1926 play *Sex*. Her subsequent arrest on charges of obscenity was not part of the act. It was real.

Mae was not only the Madonna of her day—brazenly sexual, funny, and in-your-face controversial—but was also a trail-blazer for women's rights and an advocate for minorities. "I thought white men had it their way too long," she once said, "and should stop exploiting women and blacks and gays."

In the age before feminism as we know it, Miss West presented a whole new type of female archetype. Dripping with self-confidence (and bling), Mary Jane West was master of her fate, forging her own path from Brooklyn to vaudeville to Hollywood. At least ten years older than the average starlet, she was thirty-eight when she signed a movie contract with Paramount and forty when she made *I'm No Angel*. By 1935 (at forty-two), she was one of the world's biggest stars and the highest-paid woman in the United States. Mae acted,

sang, and wrote her own material. She was an entirely self-made institution.

And she wasn't shy about announcing it. Her screen credit in *I'm No Angel* reads, "Story, Screen Play, and All Dialogue by MAE WEST." It was the biggest box-office hit of her career. Along with the films of Marlene Dietrich, *I'm No Angel* saved Paramount Pictures from bankruptcy during the bleakest years of the Depression.

Many of West's films were set in the past (often at the turn of the century), but *I'm No Angel* places her larger-than-life persona in contemporary times. Never has she been more modern or sophisticated than as lion-tamer Tira. Under the sure comedic direction of Wesley Ruggles, the film is as fresh and funny today as it was in 1933. West even beat Hollywood to the punch by casting a young, drop-dead-handsome Cary Grant as her love interest and a pre-fame

Mae West as Tira in *I'm No Angel*

"When I'm good I'm very good, but when I'm bad . . . I'm better."

—"TIRA"

Hattie McDaniel as one of her maids. Her primary maid, Beulah (Gertrude Howard), matches Tira's sassiness with back-sass of her own.

Tira dominates all the men in the picture. She even masters the king of beasts when she sticks her head inside a lion's mouth. As she ascends from small-time circus performer to big-time sensation, she encounters high-society "swells," resulting in quips galore. Just when you think she's about to run out of steam, she unleashes a fresh batch of one-liners while defending herself in the triumphant courtroom scene. When questioned about the men in her life, she delivers the legendary West-ism, "It's not the men in your life that counts, it's the life in your men." West was rife with witticisms, but there was a bite to them—her gags and double entendres often undercut society's hypocrisy regarding sexuality. They made people laugh, but also made them think.

On screen, she was bawdy but never vulgar. She could be a lady when necessary or get aggressive when it was called for. "A better dame than you once called me a liar, and they had to sew her up in twelve different places," Tira warns a society snob before shoving her out the door. After this display of brutality, she utters a line that became a national catchphrase: "Oh, Beulah, peel me a grape."

The Production Code soon spoiled the fun of Mae West. Once the Code clamped its jaws on her, she was forced to clean up her act, and her appeal fizzled. She eventually took her millions and fled the movies for live theater, where it was still acceptable to

Cary Grant and Mae West

A lobby card featuring Mae West and costar Ralf Harolde as "Slick"

be naughty. Today, West's spirit lives on in all the bodacious blondes who came later. Marilyn Monroe, Jayne Mansfield, Barbra Streisand, Debbie Harry, Bette Midler, Madonna, and Lady Gaga have all channeled Mae, whether consciously or not. "I made my way in a man's world," recalled West of her career. "What I'm proudest of is that I ... inspired [women] to stand up and walk on their own feet, not just lie on their backs."

Did You Know?

The Beatles were such fans of West that they convinced her to let them use her image on their *Sergeant Pepper's Lonely Hearts Club Band* album cover, despite her initial protests. "What would I be doing in a lonely hearts club?" she quipped.

Josephine Baker
AS "ZOUZOU"

Zouzou (1934)

***Zouzou* was more than Josephine Baker's first talkie. It was the** first major feature film to star an African American woman. It was not made in the United States, but in France. It took the big Hollywood studios years to catch up—they would not produce a sound movie with a black actress in the lead role until the 1943 musical *Cabin in the Sky,* in which Ethel Waters got top billing over Eddie "Rochester" Anderson and Lena Horne.

Zouzou is a simple rags-to-riches tale, as light as air and as predictable as Christmas. But the ecstatic charm of Josephine Baker makes it a delight to watch. As Zouzou, she is one of two orphans (one black, one white) adopted by circus performer Papa Melé. When she and her "brother" Jean grow up, Zouzou finds herself in love with him—and it's clear to see why. Jean is played by a young, roguishly cute Jean Gabin, soon to become one of French cinema's biggest deals. When Papa Melé dies and Jean is falsely accused of a crime and sent to jail, what's a girl to do? Don a skimpy costume and sing her heart out on the stage, of course. Like a saucy French version of Ruby Keeler in *42nd Street* (1933), Zouzou shimmies into the spotlight when the star of a musical revue gets sick. *Et voila!* A star is born, and her brother is saved.

Though Zouzou's feelings go unrequited (Jean loves her only as a sister), their relationship depicts something much closer to an interracial romance than would have been allowed in American movies. It is, at least, an interracial flirtation. Ultimately, the film remains a beautiful showcase for Baker's special brand of sultry *joie de vivre,* from her uninhibited dance moves to her renditions of the haunting ballad "Haiti" (performed while feathered and caged like an exotic bird) and the torch song "C'est Lui." For her grand finale number, she saunters across the stage in a golden gown as dozens of handsome, tuxedo-clad Frenchmen follow behind her, anticipating Marilyn Monroe's classic "Diamonds Are a Girl's Best Friend" number in *Gentlemen Prefer Blondes* (1953).

The character of Zouzou is idealistic and naïve, but when the men in her life let her

Josephine Baker and Jean Gabin in *Zouzou*

down—either by dying or landing behind bars—she must find the courage to save the day all by herself. In this way, the movie echoes Baker's real-life journey. "I feel the story very strongly," she said while filming *Zouzou*. "It all seems so real, so true, that I sometimes think it's my own life being played out on the sets."

As a child in St. Louis, her stepfather's unemployment led Josephine to start dancing and singing on street corners for coins to help feed her family. She'd had no training, but she taught herself by mimicking other performers and adding her own unique comic touches. "A violinist had a violin, a painter his palette. All I had was myself," she once said. Josephine sought stability by marrying at thirteen, but when her husband abandoned her, she charmed her way into a professional gig in a chorus line. By age eighteen, she was performing on New York City stages, earning $120 a week at a time when a white secretary would have averaged only $16 weekly.

La Baker became the darling of café society when she took a job in Paris, strutting her stuff in the famed Folies Bergère wearing nothing but a skirt of bananas. Her first film was the silent *Siren of the Tropics* (1927), followed by *Zouzou* and *Princess Tam-Tam* (1935). But she felt more at home on the stage than the screen. She chose to live out her life in France, where she was given star treatment everywhere, from the

Josephine Baker as Zouzou

studio to the street to high-end restaurants, regardless of race.

Josephine Baker would have been an exceptional woman in any era, but in the 1920s and 1930s, she was light-years ahead. She was photographed in a man's top hat and tails before Marlene Dietrich wore it in *Morocco* (1930); she had a string of lovers when such behavior was still taboo for women; she adopted a "Rainbow Tribe" of twelve children from various ethnic backgrounds way before Brangelina did. She also devoted her life to battling racism. "Surely the day will come," she said, "when color means nothing more than skin tone."

Did You Know?

During World War II, Baker fought the Nazi forces by doing intelligence work for France, and she was awarded the French Resistance Medal for her efforts.

DYNAMIC DAMES

> "There's only one man in Paris for me...
> and it's him."
>
> —"ZOUZOU"

Poster art for the film

Reel Role Models

If truth is stranger than fiction, then the world of movies
is even stranger. It's where truth and fiction collide, where real-life
heroines inspire cinematic renditions that don't necessarily stick
closely to the facts, but make for compelling drama all the same.
The following characters were based on real women who either
made significant contributions to society or led lives so enthralling
that their stories seemed made for the big screen. After the real
women are gone, the movies that celebrate their legacies remain.

Greta Garbo

AS "QUEEN CHRISTINA"

Queen Christina (1933)

Queen Christina of Sweden was strong willed, self-sufficient, rebellious, and a bit intimidating. It was a role Greta Garbo was born to play. Like the queen, Garbo never conformed to society's expectations. She felt burdened by her mega-stardom, always threatening to quit the movies and return to her native Sweden. Both women eventually relinquished their public acclaim to lead private lives: Christina shocked Europe by abdicating the throne at twenty-eight, and Garbo stunned Hollywood when she retired from the screen in 1941 at age thirty-six.

When she made *Queen Christina*, the woman formerly known as Greta Gustafsson had become one of the biggest names in the world. Before Cher or Madonna came along, she was known across the globe by a single moniker: Garbo. One of the few silent luminaries to smoothly transition to sound films, she had accrued the star power to select her own projects, and she chose to portray the eccentric seventeenth-century monarch.

Christina was at least two centuries ahead of her time. Her father, King Gustav II, had no sons, so he raised his daughter like a boy and declared she would someday be a "king." In fact, during her reign (from 1644 to 1654) she was often referred to as King Christina by her subjects. At a time when the average Swedish citizen could not read or write, she was highly educated, pro-arts, anti-war, openly bisexual, and fond of dressing in men's clothing. Refusing to ever marry or have children, Christina was too unconventional and headstrong to be bound by royal protocol. Garbo, believed by some to be bisexual, never married or had children either, and remained a cipher to even those closest to her.

When MGM, Garbo, and director Rouben Mamoulian resurrected Queen Christina for the screen in 1933, they used a script cowritten by Garbo's friend Salka Viertel. The result is a fascinating hybrid of historical fact and romantic embellishment, peppered with Garbo's own distinct personality traits. When Chancellor Oxenstierna (Lewis Stone) warns the queen that she may die "an old maid," she sucker-punches him

REEL ROLE MODELS |

Greta Garbo as Queen Christina in *Queen Christina*

with the now-famous retort, "I have no intention to, Chancellor. I shall die a bachelor." When she sighs, "I'm tired of being a symbol—I long to be a human being," the actress could have been speaking from her own heart. Gloriously costumed by Adrian, Garbo has rarely appeared more beautiful, or more commanding. In one scene, she enters the castle cloaked in a tailored, floor-length black coat and fur hat. When she addresses her male advisors (all of whom are wearing light colors), the contrast is striking. There's no mistaking who is in control.

Garbo flashes a smile as Queen Christina.

———◇———

"There is a freedom which is mine and which the state cannot take away ... I shall not submit! Know this, all of you."

—"QUEEN CHRISTINA"

———◇———

Of course, the real Christina would never have dreamed of abdicating for a man, but Garbo's Hollywoodized queen leaves the throne—at least in part—because of her love for sexy Spanish envoy Antonio, played by the actress's former flame John Gilbert. While traveling disguised as a man (something Christina actually did), the queen takes the last bed at an inn, then meets the Spaniard, who has no place to spend the night. The fictional scenario is milked for all its gender-bending comic possibilities. "The bed, as you know, is large," the innkeeper prompts. "You might both lie on it . . ." He practically forces Antonio and Christina to shack up. When they do, and Antonio discovers the "gloriously improbable" truth that she is a woman, they don't leave their four-poster bed for days.

Garbo is radiant in love, even breaking into peals of laughter years before advertisements for *Ninotchka* (1939) announced, "Garbo laughs!" For the celebrated final scene, when a disillusioned Christina sets sail for Spain, Mamoulian borrowed an idea from the end of Frank Capra's *The Bitter Tea of General Yen* (1932), in which Barbara Stanwyck sails for Shanghai with a cryptic look on her face. Here, Garbo's face is an expressionless mask. What does fate hold in store for the former queen? In reality, Christina appeared directionless after giving up her title, a restless wanderer unsuccessfully attempting to seize power in other countries. Garbo, too, seemed to flounder with no career or pastime to occupy her years of retirement.

Garbo initially felt embarrassed by *Queen Christina*, fearing that everyone in Sweden would blame her personally for the film's historical inaccuracies. She needn't have worried. Sweden loved her in the role as much as she loved playing it. According to co-screenwriter S.N. Behrman, Garbo "said she came closer personally to the character of Christina than any other."

Did You Know?

Bette Davis was an admirer of Greta Garbo. "Her instinct, her mastery of the machine, was pure witchcraft," Davis once said. "I cannot analyze this woman's acting. I only know that no one else so effectively worked in front of the camera."

Greta Garbo on the set with director Rouben Mamoulian and cinematographer William Daniels

Audrey Hepburn

AS "GABRIELLE VAN DER MAL, A.K.A. SISTER LUKE"

The Nun's Story (1959)

On the surface, Sister Luke doesn't seem like a very dynamic dame. Dedicated to the Catholic Church and committed to doing God's will, she quietly strives to be an obedient nun and an efficient nurse. But Gabrielle, the woman underneath the nun's habit, is not as obedient as she appears. Inside her mind, she wages a silent war, a battle between submitting to the will of the Church and exerting a will of her own. She spends virtually every moment of the two-and-a-half-hour movie fighting the urge to rebel. In the end, she can no longer restrain herself. She rebels.

With the possible exception of Ingrid Bergman, Audrey Hepburn may have been the only actress in Hollywood suitable for this role. So much of Sister Luke's conflict is played out silently—few words, few actions, just facial expressions that convey her internal struggle. Director Fred Zinnemann later wrote about why he cast Hepburn: "She was shy, coltish, and intelligent; she looked delicate, but there was a hint of iron in the jawline that signified a stubborn will. I thought she would be ideal."

Audrey's wide hazel eyes speak volumes. Growing up in the Netherlands during World War II, she had survived the German invasion and witnessed unspeakable horrors. "I am like Sister Luke in so many ways," Hepburn said, and it was true: both she and Marie Louise Habets (the real woman on whom the character was based) had been born in Belgium, both had lost their fathers, and both had brothers who were captured and sent to labor camps during the war. Using the pain of her past, Audrey delivered one of the most powerful performances of her career. She also silenced any criticism that she was simply a charming fashion plate; her hair hidden by a wimple and habit, her face virtually free of cosmetics, she set a new standard for naturalness on screen. Hepburn even suppressed her desire to look at her face while filming, as nuns are forbidden to use mirrors.

The Nun's Story began as a book by

Audrey Hepburn as Sister Luke in *The Nun's Story*

> "Dear Lord, forgive me. I can't obey anymore.
> What I do from now on is between you and me alone."
> —"SISTER LUKE"

author Kathryn Hulme, who had met former nun Habets when both were nurses in postwar Germany. While writing her story, Hulme fell in love with Habets, and the two remained romantic partners for life.

Habets was a pious and self-disciplined person whose only problem with being a nun was the oppression of individuality required when conforming to the Church, the ultimate patriarchy. As a symbolic wife of Jesus, Sister Luke's conflict is one that many women have faced for centuries: to "love, honor, and obey" their husbands. It's the blind obedience that Gabrielle cannot tolerate. In an early scene, her father (Dean Jagger) prophesies, "Gaby, I can see you poor, I can see you chaste, but I cannot see you, a strong-willed girl, obedient to those bells."

Audrey Hepburn with a local mother and child in the Belgian Congo during filming

A lobby card featuring Audrey Hepburn and Peter Finch

The atheist surgeon she assists in the Belgian Congo, Dr. Fortunati (Peter Finch), also warns her that she's not "in the mold" to be a nun. "You see things your own way," he observes. "You stick to your own ideals. You'll never be the kind of nun that your convent expects you to be." When they first meet, he catches her checking out her reflection in a pane of glass. Instead of "Hello," his first words are, "You'll say six Aves and a Pater Noster for that bit of vanity, sister." Her shame is compounded by her awareness that he is right.

It takes World War II to finally end her struggle. As a human being, Sister Luke cannot stand by impartially any more than Audrey Hepburn had as Hitler tries to destroy the world. (As a young dancer, Hepburn performed to raise money for the Resistance.) Gabrielle breaks free from the Church and its command "not to take sides" so she can work against the Third Reich. "In the end," Zinnemann has written, "she lost her fight to achieve that instant, unquestioning obedience. This was the cause of her failure as a nun and of her survival as an independent person." By forsaking her vows, Gabrielle finally becomes the independent woman who was always hiding beneath the habit.

Did You Know?

Audrey Hepburn and Marie Louise Habets became close friends during the making of the film. When Hepburn suffered serious injuries after being thrown from a horse on the set of *The Unforgiven* (1960), she sent for Habets to nurse her back to health.

Natalie Wood

AS "GYPSY ROSE LEE"

Gypsy (1962)

***Gypsy* is the saga of two dynamic dames in the guise of a** splashy musical. Louise Hovick, played by Natalie Wood, and Rosalind Russell's Rose are flamboyant and feisty ladies who share a complicated mother-daughter relationship. Mama Rose was ahead of her time—she would have made a great director, entrepreneur, or even army general. Herbie (Karl Malden) calls her "a pioneer woman without a frontier." She mercilessly dominates her two daughters as they tramp through second-rate vaudeville shows in the late 1920s and early 1930s.

Conditioned to believe she has no talent, Louise half-heartedly shuffles a few basic dance steps on stage; offstage, she is invisible, lost in the shadow of her bubbly blonde sister, song-and-dance sensation Baby June. Bulldozed by Mama for years, Louise obeys, waiting patiently to reach adulthood. When she becomes Gypsy Rose Lee, the most famous burlesque artist in history, she makes it clear that she is her own woman, severing the apron strings in no uncertain terms. "Mama, you've got to let go of me!" she explodes. "From now on, even if I flop, I flop on my own." But she doesn't cut ties completely—she knows she owes a great deal of her success to her pushy stage mother. (Off camera, Wood and Russell bonded and remained close for life.)

The real Gypsy was a deceptively smart and multi-talented woman who did so much more than seductively peel off her clothes. Known as "the girl who made the striptease respectable," she teased her way into high society. By age twenty-two, she was rolling in jewels, maids, chauffeurs, and Rolls-Royces, earning a cool thousand a week in the depths of the Depression. After going as far as she could in burlesque, she appeared in a few forgettable Hollywood films before realizing that she could write better stories herself.

Lee wrote *The G-String Murders* in 1941, a best-selling novel adapted into the 1943 movie *Lady of Burlesque,* starring Barbara Stanwyck. She sewed all her own costumes and handcrafted her stage persona as "a stripper who puts on more than she takes off," noted Lee's biographer, Karen Abbott, "and uses her wit to entice people." In 1942, *Life* magazine called her "a classic paradox: an intellectual strip-teaser." Lee published her life story, *Gypsy: A Memoir,*

Natalie Wood as Gypsy Rose Lee in *Gypsy*

Natalie Wood   Natalie Wood, Rosalind Russell, and Karl Malden

in 1957. It was quickly snatched up and turned into a hit Broadway musical by Jule Styne, Stephen Sondheim, and Arthur Laurents. Not bad for an "untalented" girl with no schooling. "Mother says I'm the most beautiful naked ass," Lee once wrote. "Well, I'm not. I'm the smartest." When her life became a movie, Lee taught Natalie Wood all her signature moves—such as a fifteen-minute glove peel—firsthand when she visited the set.

Much like Gypsy Rose Lee, Wood was a smarter, tougher cookie than she's given credit for today. A working actress since age five (who struggled under the control of her own domineering mother), at age nineteen she single-handedly took on studio head Jack L. Warner, refusing to work for four-

teen months until he gave her better roles and more freedom. Natalie won the stand-off, eventually returning to Warner Bros. with a plum role in *Splendor in the Grass*, Joan Crawford's former dressing room, and the freedom to select her next project herself. She chose *West Side Story*, which she followed with *Gypsy*.

After the triple-shot of *Splendor in the Grass*, *West Side Story*, and *Gypsy*, Wood wielded major star power in Hollywood. She presided over a team of nine agents, publicists, and lawyers that negotiated deals for her. Because it was considered unladylike in her day for women to be openly empowered, Natalie hid her business savvy behind a sweet smile. "You get tough in this business, until you get big

> "I'm having the time of my life because for the first time, it *is* my life. And I love it! I love every second of it, and I'll be damned if you're going to take it away from me!"
> —"GYPSY ROSE LEE"

enough to hire people to get tough for you. Then you can sit back and be a lady," she once said. The set of *The Great Race* in 1964 was an exception. In the film, Wood played a die-hard, marching-in-the-streets feminist, and behind the scenes, she openly fought for equality with her costars Jack Lemmon and Tony Curtis. "In all things," she told producer Martin Jurow, "I must be on the same level as Jack and Tony."

Daughter Natasha Gregson Wagner recalls her mother's subtle brand of feminism. "She had the power to wrap people around her finger with her coquettish charm, rather than using an iron fist," says Wagner. "But I saw the iron fist at times. It was right there beneath the soft exterior."

Did You Know?

Natalie Wood fondly remembered the day Gypsy Rose Lee came to the set. "She watched me for a while," Wood later wrote, "and burst into tears. It must have brought back memories." According to Lee, watching Natalie was "like going back to 1934 and coming home."

Gypsy Rose Lee visits Natalie Wood on the set.

Elizabeth Taylor
AS "QUEEN CLEOPATRA"

Cleopatra (1963)

As queen of Egypt from 51 BC to her death in 30 BC, Cleopatra VII was one of the most powerful female rulers in history. The real woman probably bore little resemblance to Elizabeth Taylor; she was scholarly, spoke at least eight languages, and was a fair and diplomatic leader. Ancient scribe Plutarch wrote that her lilting speaking voice and "irresistible charm" were what men were drawn to, not her physical beauty or sensual allure.

From the beginning, Hollywood has had its own way with Cleopatra, telling her tale with epic grandeur. In 1912, Helen Gardner—the first actor to form her own production company—produced and starred in the first feature-length *Cleopatra,* a film budgeted at a then lavish $45,000. The few fragments that survive from the 1917 version with Theda Bara (in scandalously revealing costumes) suggest an ahead-of-its-time artistry. Master of epics Cecil B. DeMille directed a stylish art-deco *Cleopatra* in 1934, with vivacious Claudette Colbert as the Queen of the Nile. British beauty Vivien Leigh played her in *Caesar and Cleopatra* in 1945.

It's a matter of opinion as to whether Elizabeth Taylor did Cleopatra *better* than her predecessors, but she certainly did it *bigger.* In 1959, before the cameras even started rolling, Liz negotiated the first ever million-dollar paycheck for an actress. After starting as an MGM contract kid known for *National Velvet* (1944) and blooming into a breathtaking young woman in films such as *A Place in the Sun* (1951), Taylor was one of Hollywood's hottest stars—and one of its most talked about. She had recently stirred up a media firestorm for breaking up the marriage of Eddie Fisher and Debbie Reynolds. Her biggest firestorm was yet to come, when she began an affair with costar Richard Burton (as Mark Antony) while still married to Fisher.

Joseph L. Mankiewicz's production of *Cleopatra* soon became just as notorious as its star. The costume changes alone—a whopping sixty-five for Taylor—were unprecedented. Its extravagant sets out-DeMilled DeMille himself. It took months of rehearsal to shoot the procession scene in which Cleopatra and her son are presented to Rome atop a giant black sphinx with three hundred slaves, several Arabian

REEL ROLE MODELS

Elizabeth Taylor as Queen Cleopatra in *Cleopatra*

> "How dare you and the rest of your barbarians set fire to my library? Play conqueror all you want, mighty Caesar! Rape, murder, pillage thousands, even millions of human beings! But neither you nor any other barbarian has the right to destroy one human thought!"
>
> —"CLEOPATRA"

horses, a few elephants, and thousands of doves in tow. This is the kind of production that bankrupted movie studios and signaled the end of Hollywood's Golden Age. It very nearly ruined Twentieth Century-Fox.

Cleopatra is a character overflowing with cinematic possibilities. A highly sexual woman who's no sex object, she is not dominated by any man, and, in fact, can outsmart them all. She's cunning and controlling, a my-way-or-the-highway lady ("There is only one way—my way," she says) with an ego big enough to match a king's. And half of *Cleopatra* gets it right. For the first two hours, Taylor's lavishly decked-out queen is a Technicolor tempest with a sharp mind and a sharper tongue. When Julius Caesar (Rex Harrison) tells her "You grow more beautiful each time I see you," without batting an eyelash, she snaps back, "And you grow balder."

For the movie's second half, after Taylor's life-threatening bout of pneumonia (plus other illnesses and personal drama) resulted in numerous shut-downs and rewrites, Cleopatra's fire fizzles into shrill histrionics. Because the film was shot in continuity, you can see the toll taken on its star: her tracheotomy scar is visible in later scenes, and she seems exhausted after two and a half years of shooting. "It was probably the most cha-

otic time of my life," Taylor told *Vanity Fair* in 1998. "It was fun and it was dark—oceans of tears, but some good times too."

But Elizabeth Taylor survived *Cleopatra*, just as she survived two stormy marriages to Burton, six other husbands, a host of health problems, and several lackluster movies. She triumphed over it all to become a philanthropist and a living legend until her death in 2011. Today, she remains a timeless icon of glamour.

The film has survived, too. When it opened, reviews were mixed and business was good, but not good enough to recoup its astronomical $44 million budget, and it was long considered a failure. Recent reappraisals have been kinder to *Cleopatra*. It's now seen as a fascinating folly with many exceptionally fine scenes and the kind of sumptuous sets and wardrobes only seen in the Hollywood of yesterday.

Did You Know?

The screenplay for *Cleopatra* was based on the script for the 1917 silent version starring Theda Bara. Twentieth Century-Fox president Spyros Skouras was reported to have found the script in the Fox archives and said, "All this needs is a little rewriting."

Top: The grand procession scene is filmed. Bottom: Richard Burton and Elizabeth Taylor

Barbra Streisand

AS "FANNY BRICE"

Funny Girl (1968)

William Wyler's screen musical *Funny Girl* is a movie of firsts.
It was Barbra Streisand's film debut, kicking off an impressive fifty-year career in motion pictures as an actress, writer, composer, and director. *Funny Girl* is also the story of Fanny Brice, considered the first woman to scale the heights of show business using her wit instead of her looks. In the 1910s, Brice set the standard still followed by contemporary standup comics. She was bold and opinionated; not a pretty face coasting on a dimpled smile, but an openly ethnic Jewish woman who wrote her own jokes, which ranged from silly to scathing (many of her gags were deemed "too offensive" and were censored). To top it all off, she sang like a bird.

Other funny females worked in teams (George Burns and Gracie Allen, for example), but Brice was a solo act who marched to her own drumbeat. "I lived the way I wanted to live," she recalled later in life, "and never did what people said I should do or advised me to do." At only seventeen, Brooklyn-born Fania Borach changed her name, dropped out of school, and hit the road with a burlesque revue; she was headlining the Ziegfeld Follies by twenty-one. Next, she eased from live theater into broadcasting, creating Baby Snooks, a hugely popular radio character from 1933 until Brice's sudden death from a stroke in 1951.

Grammy-winning songstress Streisand is also a true original. "I arrived in Hollywood without having my nose fixed, my teeth capped, or my name changed," she said, proud of her face and her background. No one would ever guess *Funny Girl* is Babs's first film—she owns it. She doesn't mimic Fanny Brice, but rather filters Brice's vibe through her own personality, which is equal parts brassy, bouncy, and vulnerable, with vocal tones as rich as honey.

At first, no one can rain on Fanny's parade. She has the chutzpah to stand up to *the* Florenz Ziegfeld when he tries to select songs for her: "One of the things I really feel definite about is choosing my own." She subverts the accepted showgirl ideal with her comic delivery and the outrageous addition of a pillow beneath her wedding gown costume. She's always ready with a joke or a smartass remark, often at her own expense.

Barbra Streisand as Fanny Brice in *Funny Girl*

But then she falls crazy in love with suave gambler Nick Arnstein (Omar Sharif) and is placed in an impossible position—a successful woman resented by her husband for earning her own money. "I intend to be the head of the family," Nick says when they marry. "It'll be the way I say or not at all." Fanny agrees, blinded by love.

At first, she chooses romance over career, leaving Ziegfeld high and dry to hop an ocean-liner with Nicky. Later, when he has a reversal of fortune and faces prison time, she's a little older and wiser; she knows she must choose career over love, as much as it hurts. She may close the film singing, "Whatever my man is, I am his forever more," but the real Fanny Brice finally divorced Arnstein when he skirted the law once too often. She couldn't be dragged down any further by a man unworthy of her.

Streisand shared her Oscar for Best Actress with the legendary Katharine Hepburn (for *The Lion in Winter* [1968]) and went on to become a legend herself as the first woman to write, produce, direct, and star in a major Hollywood movie (*Yentl* [1983]). She became known for controlling every detail of her films and firmly defended her right to do so. "Why is it men are permitted to be obsessed about their work," she once asked, "but women are only allowed to be obsessed about men?"

Both Streisand and Brice have looks that are often referred to as "unconventional,"

Barbra Streisand with her Oscar

"You think beautiful girls are going to stay in style forever? I should say not. Any minute now they're going to be out! Finished! Then it'll be my turn."

—"FANNY BRICE"

which means they don't have adorable button noses and perfect rosebud mouths. But beauty comes in all shapes and sizes. Pauline Kael put it best in the *New Yorker*: "It's been commonly said that the musical

Funny Girl was a comfort to people because it carried the message that you do not need to be pretty to succeed. That is nonsense; the 'message' of Barbra Streisand in *Funny Girl* is that talent is beauty. And this isn't some comforting message for plain people; it's what show business is all about."

Did You Know?

Screenwriter Isobel Lennart won a Writers Guild of America Award for the *Funny Girl* screenplay, which proved to be the last script she would write before her death in 1971.

Omar Sharif and Barbra Streisand

Meryl Streep
AS "KAREN BLIXEN"

Out of Africa (1985)

As one of the most prolific actors of her generation, Meryl Streep has pulled a vast array of characters from her bag of magic tricks. Yet an undeniable pattern has emerged in her career: she seems particularly drawn to strong-minded women. Karen Silkwood in *Silkwood* (1983); Gail Hartman in *The River Wild* (1994); Miranda Priestly in *The Devil Wears Prada* (2006); Margaret Thatcher in *The Iron Lady* (2011); Katharine Graham in *The Post* (2017); even her small role as women's rights advocate Emmeline Pankhurst in *Suffragette* (2015)—all of these have shaped Streep's screen image as a force to be reckoned with.

One of the most complex and compelling characters in Streep's oeuvre is the real woman who wrote the 1937 memoir *Out of Africa,* Danish author Karen Blixen, also known as Isak Dinesen. Still being unmarried in her late twenties was, according to director/producer Sydney Pollack, "a kind of humiliation" for Karen. So she made a marriage of convenience with a broke, irresponsible baron (played by Klaus Maria Brandauer)—making her a baroness—and they moved to Kenya in British East Africa.

Blixen was a proto-feminist in the 1910s who proved herself the equal of any man in intellect, fortitude, and marksmanship. Much like Sally Field's character in *Places in the Heart* (1984), when Blixen is left alone to run a farm, she rises to the occasion brilliantly, not only making the best of a tough situation but also tapping into reserves of resourcefulness and determination she didn't know she had. She also taps into a deep well of compassion. At a time when wealthy whites ruled Kenya with little concern for the native population, Blixen cares deeply for the Kikuyu people on her land and shares a close friendship with Farah (Malick Bowens), her right-hand man.

The absence of Blixen's ne'er-do-well husband allows her to pursue a romance with Denys Finch Hatton (Robert Redford), a hunter, aviator, and all-around heartbreaker. Denys lives a life free of commitments or obligations; Karen, a product of a conventional upper-crust family that expects her to have a traditional marriage and children, keeps trying to fit that mold—and to squeeze Denys into it as well.

Meryl Streep as Karen Blixen in *Out of Africa*

"The earth was made round so that we would not see too far down the road."

—"KAREN BLIXEN"

Streep has argued that the story of Karen and Denys is about something deeper than "the idea of this roaming male and the female who wants to keep him in a place." Viewers, she has observed, may have thought "that she was just trying to settle him down. But I think that Isak herself is more interesting than that."

Out of Africa is actually a love story about two people who—though they each define love differently—respect each other as equals, not as possessions. When the baron finds them together, he confronts Denys. "You might have asked," he says, man to man. "I did," Denys replies. "She said yes."

Streep portrays Blixen as a tiger. She insists on trekking through dangerous lands to deliver supplies instead of sending a man. She fights off an attacking lion single-handedly with a whip. When World War I breaks out and a lieutenant orders "women and children" be moved into town for their safety, Blixen balks. ("Is that one category or two?" she sneers.) In an

DYNAMIC DAMES

Robert Redford and Meryl Streep

era when women were expected to wear long skirts and high-necked blouses on an African safari, she's no damsel in distress. When a lion threatens to charge, Denys aims his rifle and commands her, "Drop flat and let me do it." Yeah, right. This woman isn't the kind that takes orders—she gives them. The lion charges; she doesn't drop, but pulls the trigger and shoots it herself.

Yet Karen faces a steep learning curve in the film. She doesn't realize she wants to be liberated until she has liberation thrust upon her by Denys. Only when she loses him does she begin to make peace with their unique bond. In the end, she thanks God for sharing Denys, saying, "He was not ours. . . . He was not mine." She also stops trying to dam the river on her property. She learns to let go and to love without trying to possess.

In a 1923 letter to her sister, Karen Blixen wrote, "I think it will be truly glorious when women become real people and have the whole world open before them." Today, empowered women like Meryl Streep are living the dream Blixen envisioned so long ago.

Did You Know?

Isak Dinesen's first book, *Seven Gothic Tales*, was lavishly praised upon its 1934 release in the United States. Critics and readers alike were later surprised to discover the author was female—and a baroness to boot.

Director Sydney Pollack and Meryl Streep on location in Africa

Julia Roberts
AS "ERIN BROCKOVICH"

Erin Brockovich (2000)

Erin Brockovich almost seems too good to be true. Like a comic-book hero, she's a courageous crusader for justice. Her superpowers include sticking it to the man, fighting for what's right, and telling everyone within earshot exactly what she thinks of them, profanity not spared. But the twist is, Brockovich is a real, live woman—no tights, no cape.

In the early 1990s, Brockovich was an unemployed, uneducated single mother with two ex-husbands, three kids, and sixteen dollars in her bank account. Using her ingenuity (and her prominently displayed cleavage), she transformed her own life and the lives of six hundred residents of Hinkley, California, by uncovering toxic levels of chromium in their drinking water, winning them a $333 million settlement, the largest in US history at the time.

In *Erin Brockovich,* Julia Roberts channels Erin's spitfire personality as she fights the Pacific Gas & Electric corporate machine, back-sassing her boss and breaking wardrobe guidelines the whole way. A performer with loads of natural spunk, Roberts was born to play the unapologetically ballsy Brockovich, and she scored an Oscar for her efforts. Known for her own environmental activism, the actress admired the

real woman she portrayed. "I would like to think that injustice bothers me as much as it bothers her," Roberts said in 2000. "I don't know if I would have the courage or tenacity to pursue it so doggedly as she did. I would like to think that if I was put in the situation that I would." Brockovich went above and beyond the call of duty to right the wrong that had been done to the citizens of Hinkley, advancing her own career and earning some respect in the process.

Too outspoken and unfiltered for the legal profession, Erin is a breath of fresh air in Ed Masry's staid law office, cutting through all the legalese and getting straight to the nitty-gritty. "I admit I don't know shit about shit," she yells when Ed slams a door in her face, "but I know the difference between right and wrong!" Using this kind of simple logic, she shames Ed—played by a delightfully crabby Albert Finney—into

Julia Roberts as Erin Brockovich in *Erin Brockovich*

hiring her, then shames him into taking on a David-and-Goliath case of monumental proportions. Ed and Erin's relationship is based on mutual respect and, eventually, trust. Thankfully, director Steven Soderbergh never lets them slip into a predictable father-daughter dynamic or, God forbid, one of those May-December romances Hollywood often stages between an older man and a younger woman. Ed and Erin are colleagues and friends—nothing more.

------◇------

"I'm smart, I'm hard-working, and I'll do anything. And I'm not leaving here without a job."
—"ERIN BROCKOVICH"

------◇------

Behind the scenes, several women were instrumental in bringing Erin's tale to the screen, among them screenwriter Susannah Grant and coproducer Stacey Sher. Coproducer Carla Santos Shamberg stumbled upon the true story by way of her chiropractor, who happened to be a friend of Brockovich's. The next thing she knew, the former file clerk saw her life become a Hollywood film. It was a twist of fate that usually only happens in the movies.

Soderbergh and company keep the film a personal journey, not a courtroom drama. It's human drama. And it doesn't sugar-coat the facts. It depicts the time Erin sacrificed for her job, time she could have spent with her children or in nurturing a relationship with George, her neighbor/babysitter/boyfriend. Fed up with her long working hours, George tries to guilt-trip Erin into quitting. She flatly refuses. "All I've ever done is bend my life around what men decide they need. Well, not now. I'm sorry. I won't do it," she tells him, even though it dooms their romance.

The filmmakers resist the urge for a typical chick-flick ending in which the guy returns in the final frame, all smiles, apologies, and embraces. Not here. Erin loses her man over her dedication to her career and to her cause. Judging by the look on her face when she receives her $2 million bonus at the end of the movie, she has no regrets.

The real Erin Brockovich did lose George, but in 1999, she married the right man, one supportive of her thriving career as a legal consultant and media personality. Her former boss, Ed Masry, walked her down the aisle.

Did You Know?

Erin Brockovich approved of the way Julia Roberts portrayed her, though she admitted some of the details were not completely accurate. "I think she carries off the bustier and the high heels really well," Brockovich said, "but she didn't cuss as much as I did. I can cuss up a storm, depending on my mood."

Above: Julia Roberts on set with director Steven Soderbergh. Below: Albert Finney and Julia Roberts.

Salma Hayek
AS "FRIDA KAHLO"

Frida (2002)

On the surface, *Frida* is the beautifully told story of one-of-a- kind Mexican artist Frida Kahlo. Behind the cameras, a drama unfolded that was just as fascinating and every bit as inspirational: the story of two talented women who shared a single vision and who fought the system to bring that vision to fruition.

By 2000, Mexican American actress Salma Hayek was dissatisfied with her Hollywood career. Playing sexy characters in mediocre films had made her famous, but it didn't fulfill her creatively. For six years, she had pitched the idea of producing and starring in a biopic about her idol, Frida Kahlo, but didn't encounter the right people. "The toughest thing about this movie was finding the right director," Hayek recalled. Then she met Julie Taymor, known for directing *The Lion King* on Broadway and for the visually striking film *Titus* (1999), and felt instantly that Taymor was right for the project. "The fact that she is a woman," Hayek said, "was one of the reasons why I immediately felt we see life in a similar way, and we see this character in a similar way." With Taymor on board, Hayek's dream project finally had a shot at becoming real.

Hayek and Taymor knew that there was so much more to the anguished artist than her biographers had revealed. "I think people underestimated," Hayek has opined, "how sensitive, and how passionate, and how romantic this woman is because she is strong." Many biographers also failed to convey Kahlo's humor and joy. When Taymor dug into Kahlo's life, she discovered "an exuberant woman: humorous, foul-mouthed, erotic, tenacious, fearless, and entirely feminine without sacrificing a potent sense of self-determination." Kahlo was badly injured in a trolley accident at age sixteen, leaving her unable to bear children and in chronic pain for life. She took up painting while recovering in bed, saying, "I paint self-portraits because I am so often alone, and because I am the person I know best." In her lifetime, she faced criticism for both her unconventional art and

Salma Hayek as Frida Kahlo in *Frida*

> ## "There have been two big accidents in my life, Diego: the trolley and you. You are by far the worst."
>
> —"FRIDA KAHLO"

her unconventional lifestyle as a bisexual woman in love with—and tormented by— her famously philandering husband, artist Diego Rivera.

That's a lot to squeeze into a two-hour film, and no one had yet been able to pull it off. In the 1990s, both Madonna and Jennifer Lopez announced plans to portray Frida; nothing ever materialized. But Hayek and Taymor were determined to make it happen. They took their vision to Miramax, at that time headed by Harvey and Bob Weinstein, the brother team known for fostering independent movies such as *Pulp Fiction* (1994) and *Shakespeare in Love* (1998). There, the two women were allowed to make *Frida*, an ultimately rewarding process that did not come without a price.

The real Frida Kahlo

Salma Hayek

Ashley Judd and Salma Hayek

Actress/producer Hayek later revealed that she fought off constant harassment at the hands of Harvey Weinstein, a conflict she likened to a "war." In a 2017 *New York Times* piece, she asked, "Why do so many of us, as female artists, have to go to war to tell our stories when we have so much to offer? Why do we have to fight tooth and nail to maintain our dignity?" Though battle scarred and weary, Hayek and Taymor emerged with two Oscars and a movie that achieves the near impossible: it illustrates the complexities and contradictions inherent in Frida Kahlo's life.

Drawing on the artist's letters, diaries, and paintings, Taymor paints a vivid portrait of Mexico in the 1920s through the early 1950s, filled with authentic Mexican music and surreal imagery. Colorful historical characters brought to life by Alfred Molina, Geoffrey Rush, Ashley Judd, Antonio Banderas, and Edward Norton (who made major revisions to the script) frame the hero's journey of Hayek's Frida, a wounded warrior who wills herself to walk again, teaches herself to paint, and mourns her miscarried children through her vibrant art. Despite her troubles, she still finds the passion to celebrate life and to engage in trysts with a range of famous women and men, from Josephine Baker to Leon Trotsky.

Though Frida's art was not widely acclaimed until after her death, she found the courage to keep painting. As she tells Trotsky in a scene atop the Pyramid of the Moon at Teotihuacan, Mexico, "At the end of the day, we can endure much more than we think we can." Viva Frida!

Did You Know?

For the film's opening and closing scenes, Salma Hayek shaved her upper lip in order to grow the wisp of a moustache that is visible in Frida's self-portraits and in photographs.

Keira Knightley

AS "SIDONIE-GABRIELLE COLETTE"

Colette (2018)

Known by her maiden surname, Sidonie-Gabrielle Colette

(called Gabrielle by friends and family) is one of the most celebrated authors in the history of French literature. In 1927, the respected poet Paul Claudel called her "the greatest living writer in France." Before her death in 1954, Colette had penned eighty books, including her most famous work, *Gigi*, upon which the Oscar-winning 1958 movie musical was based.

Even the "grand dame of French letters" had to start somewhere—and where she started was in the shadow of her husband, a self-inflated music critic and man-about-town known as Willy. Wash Westmoreland's 2018 biopic *Colette* traces the author's progress from "girl without a dowry" in Burgundy, France, to Willy's young wife in La Belle Époque Paris, to eventual success in her own right. As Gabrielle, Keira Knightley embodies the varied—and sometimes contradictory—qualities this woman exhibited: her keen wit, her open sexuality, her dependence on her husband, and her desire to break free from his control.

Fancying himself a "literary entrepreneur," Willy (Dominic West) hires a scribe to ghostwrite a page-turner; when his writer quits, he enlists the free labor of his wife. "You mean I can write whatever I want?" Gabrielle asks, a mischievous glint in her eye. She spends long hours crafting a semi-autobiographical tale about her experiences as a teenage girl in school. After assuring her that no one will ever want to read her work, Willy spices up *Claudine à l'école* (*Claudine at School*) with a few salacious details and sells it to a publisher, taking all the credit when it becomes an instant best seller.

Though the film is set at the turn of the twentieth century, Knightley was drawn to the story partly because Colette's struggle remains so relatable today. "The idea of someone taking credit for your work, it's such an extreme version of what so many women feel; the big bloke's in front of you, and you are sort of behind," Knightley told a reporter upon the film's release. "But I didn't feel she was a victim; she was always

Keira Knightley as Gabrielle Colette in *Colette*

a powerhouse, it was just she had to learn to find her own space and to find her own voice and to step out from behind him."

Soon, Willy is locking Gabrielle in her room and forcing her to turn out best-selling novels while he indulges in affairs with other women and is fêted throughout France as the insouciant Claudine, Gabrielle's alter-ego, becomes a national sensation. Among the first women to wear bobbed hair, years before the style became socially acceptable, Algerian actress Polaire (Aiysha Hart) inspires Gabrielle to bob her long locks. But even sporting a daring new 'do, she's still the anonymous wife of a man who passes her talent off as his.

A key player in Gabrielle's quest for independence and self-expression is Missy (Denise Gough), a marquise who dresses in men's suits and lives openly as a lesbian. Missy immediately spots that Gabrielle is the real author of the Claudine stories. As they begin a long-term liaison, Missy gently challenges Gabrielle to stand on her own two feet and to mature beyond the school-girl that Willy married. "There will come a time when you must decide," Missy says, "are you Claudine or are you Colette?"

Because she is unfaithful too, Gabrielle can tolerate Willy's infidelities, but she cannot forgive him when, without her knowledge, he sells the rights to her works for a mere five thousand francs. "Everything I thought and felt went into those books," she reminds him. "They were *me*." When she suggests they publish the next novel under both their names, Willy tells her, "No. Women writers don't sell." Presumably, he later eats these words when she divorces him, begins writing under the name Colette, and becomes the toast of the town.

"The hand that holds the pen writes history."
—"SIDONIE-GABRIELLE COLETTE"

Emerging from her husband's shadow, Colette is empowered to fearlessly forge her own path as a writer of stories about women. Her humorous, sensual tales told from the perspective of schoolgirls, courtesans, mistresses, wives, and widows served as subtle social commentaries on the traditional expectations of women, making Colette an ultra-modern role model. "It's about time," as Keira Knightley observes, "that we saw the world through women's eyes."

Did You Know?

When Colette's *Gigi* was first adapted for the stage in 1951 by writer, dramatist, and all-around wit Anita Loos, Colette herself selected a young, untrained actress to play her Gigi. Her name was Audrey Hepburn.

Top: Dominic West and Keira Knightley. Bottom: Colette draws from personal memories to write her novels.

Big Bad Mamas

In real life, being a mother may be the world's hardest and most rewarding job. In the male-dominated film industry, however, women are too often relegated to predictable roles as girlfriends, wives, and mothers, with little in-depth character development of their own. But, with some attention on the part of writers, directors, and actresses, wives and mothers can be the most fascinating characters in the story. The following movie mamas are strong, they're fiercely protective, and they're never one-dimensional.

Joan Crawford

AS "MILDRED PIERCE"

Mildred Pierce (1945)

In 1943, at age thirty-eight, Joan Crawford was unceremoniously dropped from the studio that had groomed and nurtured her for nearly twenty years, Metro-Goldwyn-Mayer. Though she negotiated a new contract at Warner Bros., her future didn't look too rosy. Popular opinion was that her best years were behind her; she had even been labeled "box office poison" by theater-chain owner Harry Brandt in 1938. No good scripts came her way, and she knew that her career would be finished unless she scored an absolutely stellar part. It would be two years, Joan recalled, "before I could find a story I believed in."

Enter the ultimate career gal, Mildred Pierce, James M. Cain's waitress-turned-restaurateur who builds an empire of fried chicken and homemade pies to please her spoiled-rotten daughter, Veda. Mildred is a working-class single mother—hardly the kind of glamour girl Crawford had become famous for at MGM—but it was an intense, complex role, one that would test her acting chops and show the world that she was back on top. She wanted it badly.

Director Michael Curtiz had no interest in casting Crawford. He quickly changed his tune, however, when she submitted to a screen test—the ultimate indignity for a star of her caliber—and he was confronted with her professionalism and willingness to take direction. When Eve Arden was cast as Mildred's business partner and stalwart gal pal Ida, the movie boasted two dynamic dames for the price of one. One of many changes made in the adaptation from book to screenplay was Ida's character: in the novel she's married, while in the film she's a single businesswoman and resident sharpest-knife-in-the-drawer.

Although Ranald MacDougall got all the credit (and the Oscar nomination for Best Screenplay) after his rewrites, the sprawling Cain novel had first been wrangled into a script by Catherine Turney, one of the few female screenwriters on staff at Warner Bros. "They were a male-oriented studio not particularly predisposed to women writers," Turney later said. "We were seen as a necessary evil and were seldom paid as

Joan Crawford as Mildred Pierce in *Mildred Pierce*

Joan Crawford, Eve Arden as Ida, and Chester Clute (as Mildred's accountant)

much as the men." Turney excelled at penning spot-on dramatic dialogue for women, such as the classic confrontation when Veda (Ann Blyth) lashes out at her mother: "You think now you've made a little money you can get a new hairdo and turn yourself into a lady, but you can't, because you'll never be anything but a common frump whose father lived over a grocery store and whose mother took in washing."

Crawford's acting in this scene might be the rawest she's ever done. When her face is slapped by Veda (Joan insisted on an authentic smack), she is taken aback, losing her balance and stumbling backward. As the camera zooms in on her face and she slowly rises, we catch a glimpse of the wounded pride, the fierce tenacity inside the real Joan Crawford. Her eyes flash with a rage so visceral it can't even be voiced.

All Mildred can say is, "Get out, Veda. Get your things out of this house right now before I throw them into the street and you with them. Get out before I kill you." Veda knows her mama means business. She turns and runs.

Though driven by blind maternal instinct, Crawford's Mildred is at once more aspirational (in her tailored suits with those famous shoulder pads) and more relatable than the bedraggled heroine of the book. As Henry Hart observed in *Films in Review*, "Crawford gave *Mildred Pierce* a reality it might have otherwise lacked, because it was her own life in some ways, a strong woman struggling against misfortune and the wrong men." This character not only echoed the star's life as she clawed her way from being Texas-born Lucille LeSueur to Hollywood royalty Joan Crawford, but it

Zachary Scott and Joan Crawford shoot a nightclub scene.

> "You look down on me because I work for a living, don't you? You always have. Alright, I work. I cook food and sell it and make a profit on it, which, I might point out, you're not too proud to share with me."
>
> —"MILDRED PIERCE"

echoed the lives of many average women who went to see her films. It was one of the top-grossing movies of the year.

Mildred Pierce saved Joan Crawford from the brink of extinction and established a paradigm for the next phase of her stardom; she would spend at least a decade playing variations of the Mildred type. The film also earned her the only Academy Award in her forty-year career, which she claimed was "more of a lifetime Oscar which they gave for the sum of the best of my films, *A Woman's Face* and *Grand Hotel* and a few others. With extra points for sticking around so long."

Did You Know?

When Kate Winslet took the reins as Mildred Pierce in a 2011 miniseries, she deliberately avoided watching the 1945 film. "I would have felt under incredible pressure," Winslet said, to be "as good as Joan Crawford."

Gene Tierney

AS "LUCY MUIR"

The Ghost and Mrs. Muir (1947)

"I've never had a life of my own," declares Lucy Muir, a young widowed mother, to her weepy mother-in-law and resentful sister-in-law. "There's been Edwin's life, and yours.... Never my own."

Early in *The Ghost and Mrs. Muir*, Lucy decides to lead her own life, despite the demands of her dreadful in-laws and the oppressive rules of Edwardian society. She exchanges her black mourning dress for light-colored clothing, rents a cottage by the sea, and moves in with her daughter, Anna (played by an eight-year-old Natalie Wood in her third screen role), and housekeeper, Martha. Though she's a prim, proper lady who doesn't curse, shout, or march in the streets for equal rights, in her own quiet way, Lucy is a radically independent woman.

Defying the advice of her skittish real-estate agent, Lucy settles into Gull Cottage, even though it's inhabited by the spirit of salty sea captain Daniel Gregg, played by an equally salty Rex Harrison. At first, Captain Gregg thinks he can frighten her away. He clearly has no idea who he's dealing with; Lucy is thrilled to discover the specter. "Haunted," she says with a grin. "How per-fectly fascinating." Soon, the ghost and Mrs. Muir are behaving like a married couple. She even ends up—gasp!—sleeping in the captain's bedroom, where he spies on her as she undresses. Of course, he's only a spirit, so it's not really breaking the Production Code (wink, wink), but there's an undeniable sexual undercurrent to their relationship.

Daniel encourages Lucy to stand up for herself. He nicknames her "Lucia" ("a name for an Amazon, for a queen," he says) and even devises a plan to help her become financially independent. Giving new meaning to the term *ghostwriting*, Daniel dictates his salacious life story, which Lucy turns into a best-selling novel so she can earn royalties, purchase the house, and support herself and her daughter for the rest of their days. In the process, he teaches her some impolite language, which she puts to good use. When the in-laws drop by, she sends them away with a hearty "Please be good enough to shove off."

Gene Tierney as Lucy Muir in *The Ghost and Mrs. Muir*

> "I won't be shouted at!
> Everyone shouts at me
> and orders me about and
> I'm sick of it, do you hear?
> Blast. Blast, blast!"
>
> —"LUCY MUIR"

The widow and the captain make the perfect couple until that great scoundrel of the silver screen, George Sanders (as duplicitous slimeball Miles Fairley), spoils their supernatural romance. Miles loathes children and patronizes Lucy ("Is it a cookbook?" he asks of her manuscript), whereas Captain Gregg—even after he disappears—respects Lucy's child and her space, waiting patiently for her just beyond the realm of the living. That's what's so beautiful about their unconventional love affair: ironically, it feels more authentic than many a celluloid romance because it's a spiritual and mental bond they share, not merely one of the flesh. He cares enough to give her the ultimate gift: the freedom to live the life she chooses.

Though *The Ghost and Mrs. Muir* was just another studio assignment for Joseph L. Mankiewicz, he directs this "woman's

Joseph L. Mankiewicz, Gene Tierney, and Rex Harrison on set

picture" with sparkle and style, keeping the female viewpoint firmly intact. The novel it was based on was written by R.A. Dick, whom many believed to be a man. In fact, it was the nom-de-plume of Josephine Aimée Campbell Leslie, a woman who—like the character she created—changed her fortune by publishing a successful book for the first time in midlife.

With her composed manner and beauty that's almost otherworldly, Gene Tierney makes us totally buy that she's a turn-of-the-century maiden who falls in love with a ghost. She was an actress of greater range than is often recognized; just two years before she played Lucy, she was spellbindingly convincing as a cold-blooded murderer in *Leave Her to Heaven* (1945). Offscreen, Tierney's life was marred by tremendous adversity. Her dreams of motherhood were tarnished when she gave birth to a baby girl who was severely mentally impaired—the result of exposure to German measles during pregnancy. Later, she was forced to leave Hollywood (and her second daughter, Tina) behind for five years as she struggled to regain her mental health in a series of sanitariums, some of which employed primitive methods like electroshock therapy and ice-water baths.

But, unlike many tragic Hollywood figures, Gene proved to be stronger than her troubles. She survived her difficult years and

Rex Harrison and Gene Tierney in character

learned, as she later wrote, "that the mind is the most beautiful part of the body."

Did You Know?

Gene Tierney hobbled through most of the film with a broken foot; her limp is even visible in a few scenes. She had injured herself running up a flight of stairs to visit the newly born granddaughter of Fanny Brice.

Sophia Loren

AS "CESIRA"

Two Women (1960)

She may be an uneducated, working-class grocer, but Cesira in Vittorio De Sica's *Two Women* is blessed with a wealth of wisdom and an indomitable sense of pride. When her shop is torn apart by bombing in World War II–era Rome, she packs up her twelve-year-old daughter, Rosetta (Eleanora Brown), and flees for the safety of the countryside, a fat roll of cash nestled in her ample bosom. Tragically, she learns that no place is safe in wartime.

On the way, she's grabbed and/or leered at by every male in sight. "Nobody can treat me like that," she yells at a man who slaps her behind. "I'm nobody's property!" She risks her life by threatening a high-ranking officer with a rock when he tries to pimp out Rosetta to his regiment of men. She and her daughter are nearly gunned down by a fighter plane. And that's only the first twenty minutes of the movie. When a train passenger asks who she's angry at, she snaps, "Everyone." Cesira is angry at her deceased husband, at Mussolini, at Hitler, at all the men who have made her life a living hell. She's angry because, in a culture steeped in sexism, she has no power to fight back. "If I was a man," she cries in frustration, "I'd go out and shoot them all, the dirty murderers!" But, as one character mansplains when

Cesira explodes with rage at a German officer, "she's only a woman."

Sophia Loren was showered with awards for her emotionally charged performance. Besides snaring a British Academy Award, a David di Donatello, and a Best Actress prize at Cannes, she made history as the first Oscar recipient (Best Actress) to win for a performance in a foreign-language film. Only in her twenties, she rips up the screen as the world-weary mom of a tween. "This girl is a saint. I'm not even worthy to be her mother," Cesira tells Michele (Jean-Paul Belmondo), an intellectual pacifist and one of the few gentlemen she encounters on her adventure. When he asks Cesira if she ever thinks of love, she replies, "My daughter is enough for me." This mother's love for her child is so all-consuming there's no room in her heart for anyone else.

Sophia Loren as Cesira in *Two Women*

> "Do you know what they have done, those heroes that you command? Do you know what your great soldiers have done in a holy church, under the eyes of the Madonna? Do you know what they have done!"
>
> —"CESIRA"

Believing they'll be safe in a bombed-out church, mother and daughter take refuge, only to be violently attacked and raped by a gang of soldiers. Cesira may recover, but her traumatized Rosetta will never be the same. It's one of the most gut-wrenching scenes in cinema—and yet it's only a build-up to Sophia's tour de force moments, when she hurls rocks (and epithets) at a jeep of soldiers and delivers the spanking of a lifetime to Rosetta, unleashing a torrent of pent-up fury over her daughter's loss of innocence.

There have been many films illustrating the effect of World War II on women's lives; *Mrs. Miniver* (1942), *So Proudly We Hail!* (1943), and *Since You Went Away* (1944) were a few of the major Hollywood productions. But rarely has a movie provided such a harrowing, unflinching look at war's impact on women and children. Even compared to modern films, *Two Women* feels brutally honest, largely because of Sophia Loren's sublime characterization.

Loren drew upon her own personal pain from growing up in war-torn Italy. "When I think of my first memories," she wrote in her 2014 autobiography, "I can hear the bombs falling and exploding and the anti-aircraft sirens wailing. I can feel the hunger pangs and see the cold darkness of those dreadful nights of war." Loren recalled her mother begging for a crust of bread, like Cesira does, to feed her children. In 1957, she "devoured" Alberto Moravia's novel *Two Women*, feeling that "it was about me and my mother."

In the book, Cesira is thirty-five and Rosetta eighteen. Loren was twenty-six—too young for the mother and too old for the daughter. But De Sica wanted her in the film. When Anna Magnani, the actress originally slated for Cesira, refused to play Sophia's mother, De Sica cast Loren instead and made the daughter younger. He tailored the whole film specifically for his leading lady. "It was the most difficult role I'd played in my entire career," Loren has said; it has also been her most acclaimed. In an incredible sixty-year career, Cesira remains the gold standard, the ultimate Italian mama of the cinema.

Did You Know?

In 1989, Sophia Loren reprised her role as Cesira in the Italian made-for-television movie *Running Away,* a retelling of *Two Women*.

Top: Sophia Loren and Eleanora Brown. Bottom left: Cesira prays for the war to end. Bottom right: Loren makes history at the 34th annual Academy Awards ceremony in 1962.

Anne Bancroft

AS "MRS. ROBINSON"

The Graduate (1967)

"And here's to you, Mrs. Robinson. Jesus loves you more than you will know." Never mind that Paul Simon originally intended the song for Eleanor Roosevelt ("Here's to you, Mrs. Roosevelt") until Mike Nichols convinced him to repurpose the lyrics for *The Graduate*. It's still a Grammy-winning classic that lovingly memorializes Anne Bancroft's seasoned seductress, and its catchy chorus softens some of the harsh treatment her character receives in the movie.

Four years before she played Mrs. Robinson, Anne Bancroft won an Oscar for *The Miracle Worker* (1962), in which she portrayed one of the toughest, most determined women in history: Annie Sullivan, who persevered through tremendous obstacles to teach the deaf and blind Helen Keller to communicate. When Nichols cast Bancroft as the older woman who coerces young Benjamin Braddock (Dustin Hoffman) into his first sexual encounter, the director got more than he bargained for. She doesn't just seduce Benjamin; with her potent mix of strength, sophistication, and earthy allure, she seduces the audience.

A natural predator in a leopard-skin coat and silk stockings, Mrs. Robinson not only teaches Ben a thing or three about sex, but also has depth and mystery. We never even discover her first name. She's ultra-cool and says tantalizingly little. Her daughter,

the nice, sheltered Elaine (Katharine Ross), seems hopelessly bland by comparison.

Before long, Ben learns a few details about this lady. Not only do she and Mr. Robinson sleep in separate bedrooms, but she also relinquished her own personal aspirations when she was Ben's age. Arguably, the most poignant moment in the comedy is when she reveals she majored in art, yet now claims to know nothing about it. When Ben assumes that she "kind of lost interest in it over the years," a veil of regret falls over her face as she sighs, "Kind of." She's mourning the life she could have had if she hadn't gotten pregnant, forcing her to quit school and get married. "All the dreams that she had for herself, and the talent," Anne Bancroft has pointed out, "none of that could happen anymore."

Bancroft fueled her desperate housewife with a deep well of frustration. When

---

Anne Bancroft as Mrs. Robinson in *The Graduate*

Mrs. Robinson forces a promise out of Benjamin, played by Dustin Hoffman.

Nichols first began directing her in rehearsals, she understood instantly what drove her character: anger. She played the whole film with, in her words, a "terrible rage" simmering just beneath the immaculately dressed surface.

Just as the mystery of Mrs. Robinson begins to unfold, Ben screws up everything by taking Elaine out on a date. Mrs. R. may be a flawed mother, but you can't fault her here—she forbids it, for Elaine's sake and her own. What woman would be okay with her summer fling romancing her own daughter? Ben even admits he had "no interest in taking her out" until Mrs. Robinson ordered him not to. Soon, Ben not only breaks his promise not to date Elaine, but also ends up stalking her and becomes obsessed with the idea of marrying her.

> "Listen to me very carefully, Benjamin. You are not to see Elaine again ever. Those are my rules, is that clear? I can make things quite unpleasant."
>
> —"MRS. ROBINSON"

When Elaine appears, the plug is abruptly pulled on Mrs. Robinson and her perspective. We're left to imagine how hurt

Anne Bancroft on the set of *The Graduate*

she must have been over Ben's betrayal and how much their affair damaged her relationship with her daughter. She becomes the villain of the movie; the audience now roots for Ben and Elaine and is expected to view Mrs. Robinson as—in the words of Ben—"a broken-down alcoholic."

Today, the tide has turned. History has been kinder to Mrs. Robinson than to those confused, privileged (read: spoiled) college kids Ben and Elaine. Roger Ebert probably spoke for many when he re-reviewed *The Graduate* for its thirtieth anniversary in 1997 and observed that Mrs. Robinson, for him, had become "the most sympathetic and intelligent character" in the film and that Ben seemed like "an insufferable creep." Today, when women in their forties are considered more desirable than they were fifty years ago, Mrs. Robinson would be a dream come true for a directionless twentysomething with too much time on his hands.

Thanks to the inner fire Anne Bancroft brings to Mrs. Robinson, she not only steals the movie but also walks away looking better and better in hindsight. Perhaps Ebert summed it up best: "Seen today, *The Graduate* is a movie about a young man of limited interest, who gets a chance to sleep with the ranking babe in his neighborhood, and throws it away in order to marry her dorky daughter."

The one ray of hope for Bancroft's character comes near the end, when her blustering husband announces they are divorcing. Here's hoping that Mrs. Robinson finally found happiness as a hot divorcée.

Did You Know?

Anne Bancroft was only thirty-five in *The Graduate*, a mere six years older than Dustin Hoffman. Makeup and harsh lighting were used to make her look more mature.

Linda Hamilton

AS "SARAH CONNOR"

The Terminator (1984) *and*
Terminator 2: Judgment Day (1991)

From her introduction in *The Terminator* to her first appearance in *Terminator 2: Judgment Day*, Sarah Connor does a complete 180. She starts as a mousy hamburger-joint waitress being stalked by a cyborg and transforms into a ripped, tough-as-nails fighting machine powerful enough to rival the Terminator himself. Her character arc is off the charts.

Like Ridley Scott's *Alien* had in 1979, *The Terminator* starts as a fairly standard sci-fi thriller, then veers in a subversive feminist direction. Its subtext is that of a woman becoming empowered. Sarah Connor is the true protagonist, not either of the two men who fight over her—the titular Terminator (Arnold Schwarzenegger) or Kyle Reese (Michael Biehn). Destined to bear a child who will someday save the post-apocalyptic world from being phased out by machines, Sarah and her son, John, are literally mankind's hope for the future.

The male-fantasy element inherent in so many action movies is hijacked and reversed in *The Terminator*. A cute guy traveling all the way from the future to find one special lady falls more into the realm of *female* fantasy. In a sense, Reese's sole purpose in life is to become Sarah's lover; he's never even been with another woman, and he dies after completing his mission to father her child. Now that's truly a one-woman man! In the tradition of Detective Mark McPherson (Dana Andrews) in *Laura* (1944), Reese falls in love with Sarah's photograph and goes to great lengths to protect her once he encounters the real thing. By the time he is seriously injured near the end, Sarah has assumed the position of the hero, pulling the man to his feet and barking "On your feet, soldier!" like a drill sergeant.

In creating Sarah, writer/director James Cameron took some inspiration from his own mother, Shirley, a macho mama who was in the Canadian Women's Army Corps; in her spare time, she went target shooting and raced stock cars. From day one, Cameron has placed strong female characters

Linda Hamilton as Sarah Connor in *The Terminator*

front and center in his movies, often to the detriment of the males, who sometimes appear brow-beaten by the female element (see *The Abyss* [1989] for details). "Sarah Connor was not a beauty icon," said Cameron in 2017, defending his character as a feminist role model. "She was strong, she was troubled, she was a terrible mother, and she earned the respect of the audience through pure grit." She also won the respect of the director, who later married (and divorced) his leading lady.

As he did for Sigourney Weaver in *Aliens* (1986), Cameron makes Linda Hamilton into a full-blown action hero in *Terminator 2*, the sequel released seven years after the original. Early in the film, when Sarah is incarcerated, Reese appears in a dream, cheerleading her into action (usually a woman's job in movies). "You're strong, Sarah," he tells her. "Stronger than you ever thought you could be." And it's true. After years of combat training and pumping iron, she nearly escapes a maximum-security institution on her own using a paperclip, MacGyver-style. She growls "Don't fuck with me!" to the security guards poised to attack her, and when her psychiatrist wails, "You broke my arm!" her response is ice cold: "There are 215 bones in the human body. That's one." Sarah ferociously guards the life of her son (Edward Furlong) like a mother lion, but isn't exactly a warm and fuzzy mom.

This time around, she's even scarier than Schwarzenegger.

Reprogrammed to be benevolent, the Terminator is as much of a loving parent to John as Sarah is. Instead of a menacing "I'll be back," he now says things like "Trust me" and "I need a vacation," phrases that don't exactly strike terror in anyone's heart. Sarah and the T-800 actually make a great team. While fighting to destroy the newfangled liquid metal T-1000 cyborg, she

Linda Hamilton in *Terminator 2: Judgment Day*

Linda Hamilton, James Cameron, Joe Morton, and Arnold Schwarzenegger on the set of *Terminator 2: Judgment Day*

> "You think you're so creative. You don't know what it's like to really create something, to create a life, to feel it growing inside you. All you know how to create is death and destruction."
>
> —"SARAH CONNOR"

covers her partner with her handgun while he reloads his shotgun. John compares the two, observing that both have "no sense of humor" and "could lighten up."

Sarah Connor may not be June Cleaver, but she's one of the strongest, bravest moms so far in the history of the movies. As an unmarried, gun-toting, action-hero mother, she deconstructs Hollywood's conventional notions of women and motherhood, making her years ahead of her time.

Did You Know?

The psychotic tinge Sarah took on in *Terminator 2* was Linda Hamilton's idea. When James Cameron called her to discuss the sequel, Hamilton told him "she didn't want to be the little waitress that she played the first time," Cameron recalled in 2017. "She said, 'I want to be crazy.'"

Fatal Femmes

Caution: These women are hazardous to your health.
Ever since "vamp" Theda Bara uttered the immortal line
"Kiss me, my fool" (silently, of course) in the 1915 melodrama
A Fool There Was, dangerous females have been a cinematic staple.
Though they may or may not be capable of cold-blooded murder,
these lethal ladies are not above luring men to their demise. Some-
times they have good reasons—vengeance, self-defense—but watch
out. This kind of girl shoots first and asks questions later.

Hedy Lamarr

AS "MADELEINE DAMIAN"

Dishonored Lady (1947)

In the noirish "woman's picture" *Dishonored Lady*, Hedy Lamarr cuts an impressive figure as self-assured art editor Madeleine Damian. Behind the scenes, the awe-inspiring actress, inventor, and producer hoped this examination of a career girl with a dark side would show the world she was more than just the "Most Beautiful Woman in Films."

Madeleine plays by a man's rules. At work, she ambushes a group of men, reminding them in no uncertain terms who their superior is: "Am I running my department or am I not?" One of her advertisers, Felix Courtland (John Loder), tells Madeleine she has "a man's mind," to which she retorts, "Why not? I do a man's work." Navigating a lion's den where the guys call women "sweetheart" and "baby," she must maintain a tough veneer to survive. The whole building teems with gossip about her sex life; even after business hours, she still can't escape judgy men. "It's awfully hard making love to a woman who makes more money than I do," complains Jack Garet (William Lundigan), a lower-ranking employee, as they foxtrot on the dance floor.

Underneath Madeleine's confident façade swirls a torrent of emotions that she numbs with work, sex, sleeping pills, and booze. When she encounters (by crashing her car into his house) a psychiatrist who understands that she's using these vices to avoid herself, she quits her job, develops a healthier lifestyle, and falls in love with David (Dennis O'Keefe), a fellow lodger in her boarding house. Madeleine tries her best to conform to David's view of her—as the wholesome ideal of postwar femininity—but her past comes knocking one night when she's coaxed into a nightclub by an old friend. She downs one too many cocktails, is seduced into Courtland's apartment, and becomes suspect number one in his murder.

The instant he learns she's mixed up in a scandal, David turns against Madeleine. At the trial, her character is publicly assassinated; she's "irresponsible," "weak," and "heartless." Thankfully, in the final scenes, her psychiatrist comes to Madeleine's

Hedy Lamarr as Madeleine Damian in *Dishonored Lady*

defense, and she is ultimately redeemed—not only publicly, but in David's eyes as well.

Dishonored Lady began as the salacious story of a nymphomaniac who commits murder to prevent her fiancé from discovering her wanton past (inspired by a notorious true crime from 1857). Lamarr—bored with playing roles that required her to do little more than wear bejeweled gowns and look exotic—purchased the material, partnered with producers Jack Chertok and Hunt Stromberg, and looked forward to being in control for a change. "I know if I don't do a good job," she said during production, "I'll have no one to blame but myself."

Hedy Lamarr gets into costume for the film.

> "As a blackmailer, you're pitiful. Go on, tell him what a rat I am, and you are, and he is! Go on, use my phone if you want, and my desk, and my office. I'm through with all of them!"
>
> —"MADELEINE DAMIAN"

But that pesky Production Code forced major changes on the script, prohibiting Madeleine from killing Courtland and barring direct references to her sex addiction. Lamarr's character went from a dangerously sexy femme fatale to a promiscuous, unhappy lady with vaguely defined problems. In its review, *Modern Screen* squawked, "If you're a beautiful woman with a fascinating job, plenty of money, and dozens of men in love with you, what you need, it seems, is a psychiatrist." Though it's never stated in the dialogue, a subtext implies that Madeleine's unhappiness may stem from feeling constantly judged by a male-dominated society.

Dishonored Lady was a disappointment for its star. Possibly due to the censoring of story elements, or simply because this type of melodramatic female-driven film was going out of style in the late 1940s, the movie lost money and did little for Lamarr's lagging career.

Morris Carnovsky, as psychiatrist Dr. Caleb, advises Madeleine.

Like Madeleine Damian, Lamarr was often prejudged and misunderstood. A multi-talented woman of intense intellectual curiosity, Austrian-born Hedwig Kiesler might have been a renowned inventor had she been taken more seriously. After escaping her controlling husband (as the Nazis encroached upon Europe) to become one of MGM's top leading ladies, in 1942 she patented a radio-controlled torpedo that operated by frequency hopping—the same technology we use today for cell phones and Wi-Fi. Though they never credited or paid her, the US military has been using her invention since 1957.

As an actress, Lamarr was underutilized by Hollywood, where her extraordinary beauty was as much a curse as a blessing. Her costar (and third husband) John Loder expressed it perfectly in 1944: "The trouble is that her looks belie her brains. You see, people don't expect her to be intelligent as well as beautiful."

Did You Know?

Hedy was a hands-on producer, personally supervising every detail from wardrobe fabrics to screen-credit typeface. In 1946 she said, "I decided to become a producer so that I would have a voice not only in script and casting and what kind of a picture I would appear in, but in small things."

Ida Lupino

AS "LILY STEVENS"

Road House (1948)

"Silly boy," rasps Lily Stevens after slapping the hell out of
Pete (Cornel Wilde), the manager in the dive where she works. It's the ultimate takedown
of his condescending, dismissive attitude toward her, and it stops him cold. Though Pete
pretends to hate Lily, this may be the moment he starts to fall in love with her. The audience
is way ahead of him. We've been in love with this sass-mouthed dame since the first scene
of Jean Negulesco's classic noir *Road House*, when she sits shuffling cards, bare-legged and
barefooted, with gams to kill for and her lit cigarette burning a hole in the table.

Lily is a gravel-throated songbird in a
two-bit roadhouse, but she performs "One
for My Baby (and One More for the Road)"
with such effortless charm that she knocks
everyone out: both guys she works for, and
even the cashier, Susie (Celeste Holm), who
has a crush on the hunky Pete and tries
her best to despise Lily. The owner, Jefty
(Richard Widmark), hires Lily, then
decides to marry her without even pausing
to get her input. "She's a funny girl—
independent," Pete warns Jefty. "Yeah,
she's independent," Jefty replies, "but all
gals want the same thing, Pete. A guy to
take care of them." It's with this same
cluelessness that the narcissistic Jefty
announces to Lily, "I've got news for
you....We're getting married." When she
takes a shine to Pete instead, she's a lady
caught in a lethal love triangle.

Ida Lupino's frank, free-spirited sex
appeal is a refreshing change of pace for the
late 1940s, when most female characters
were either too good to be bad or too bad for
their own good. Here, the lovely "poor man's
Bette Davis" (as Lupino described herself)
manages to hit that sweet spot in the middle.
She's hard-boiled, always quick with a put-
down or a wisecrack. When she stands extra
close to Wilde and murmurs, "I think I get
the idea," after rolling a strike in the bowling
alley, she ain't just talking about knocking
down pins; she shoots him a look that oozes
seduction. Yet Lily is the rare femme fatale
who acts as both seductress and hero when
she saves the lives of every decent person in
the film by killing the bad guy in the end.

Lily Stevens in *Road House* is Lupino's
signature role in a career that spanned five
decades both in front of and behind the

Ida Lupino takes a break on the set of *Road House*.

> "Listen, when I want to leave, I'll let you know. I came out here with a contract, I needed the dough. And I'm going to collect every nasty little cent of it, maybe more. Who knows? Before I'm through, *you* might be running for the depot."
>
> —"LILY STEVENS"

camera. She owns the movie, singing in her own distinctive cigarette-smoked alto (at a time when dubbed singing voices were the norm) and getting top billing over her male costars. In fact, Ms. Lupino was the driving force behind the film, shrewdly purchasing the story rights and negotiating a starring deal with Fox. "This is exactly the kind of picture I've wanted to do for a long time," she said in 1948. "It has everything I've looked for the last year—hard-hitting drama, action, and a love story with a completely new twist."

The following year, she made history when she coscripted and produced the ripped-from-the-headlines story of illegitimate pregnancy *Not Wanted* (1949). It wasn't the film that was so exceptional; it was the fact that, when director Elmer Clifton had a heart attack early in the production and required time off to recover, Lupino settled right into the director's chair and never looked back. Soon she became literally the only female director in Hollywood; in 1950, the Directors Guild consisted of thirteen hundred

Lily performs a song.

Ida Lupino behind a home-movie camera

Cornel Wilde and Ida Lupino

men, and one Ida. (Dorothy Arzner, by then retired, had preceded her in the 1930s and 1940s.)

Her director's chair read: "Mother of us all," a more appropriate sobriquet than anyone probably realized at the time. Considered the godmother of today's independent filmmakers, Lupino bucked the system at every turn, refusing to be intimidated by the all-powerful studios. "If Hollywood is to remain on the top of the film world, I know one thing for sure—there must be more experimentation with out-of-the-way film subjects," she once said. And she took it upon herself to solve this problem, making low-budget pictures that tackled taboo subject matter like rape and sexual harassment, usually from a female perspective. How did she earn her all-male crew's respect in an era when sexism was commonplace? "You do not tell a man," she advised. "You suggest to him."

Did You Know?

Margaret Gruen coauthored (with Oscar Saul) the original story *The Dark Love*, on which *Road House* was based. She contributed to the screenplays of *Mildred Pierce* (1945) and a few other films before being blacklisted when she was named as a member of the Communist Party in 1952.

Dorothy Dandridge

AS "CARMEN JONES"

Carmen Jones (1954)

Dorothy Dandridge was a born performer. While pregnant with her, Dandridge's mother left her father for a woman, and the two ladies raised Dorothy and her older sister, Vivian, to be showbiz kids. With no formal education to speak of, Dandridge developed into a talented, charismatic singer/dancer/actress who was privately tormented by insecurities. She hid her demons beneath a beautiful and poised exterior. In fact, she was so poised that she had a hard time convincing director Otto Preminger that she could play the lusty lead in his audacious all-black-cast musical *Carmen Jones*.

"Before I was tested, Mr. Preminger told me I seemed too sweet, too regal, that he didn't think I'd do," Dandridge told the *New York Times* in 1954. But she gave Preminger the hard sell, telling him, "Look, I know I can do it. I understand this type of woman. She's primitive, honest, independent, and real—that's why other women envy her." She not only won the part, but won over Preminger, who became her lover during the production.

Conceived for the stage by Oscar Hammerstein II in 1943, *Carmen Jones* is a jazzy update of Georges Bizet's 1875 opera *Carmen*. Seen through today's lens, the film's portrayal of African Americans is ambivalent. On the one hand, it respects the importance of the characters' lives; on the other hand, its "dat" and "dem" vernacular and racial stereotypes were crude and outmoded even when it was made. The movie's saving grace is its stellar cast: Carmen's love interest is a young Harry Belafonte, and her girlfriends are played by Pearl Bailey and Diahann Carroll.

As Carmen, Dorothy Dandridge is electrifying. She's a real "hot bundle" from the moment she appears, sauntering in to her job at the parachute factory in a low-cut black blouse and flaming red-orange wrap skirt. When this hot-blooded mama is arrested for "interfering with the war effort" (starting a catfight with a coworker), fate throws army corporal and aspiring

Dorothy Dandridge as Carmen Jones in *Carmen Jones*

> "Maybe you ain't got the message yet, but Carmen's one gal nobody puts on a leash. No man's gonna tell me when I can come and go. I gotta be free or I don't stay at all."
>
> —"CARMEN JONES"

pilot Joe (Belafonte) in her path; he must drive her to prison. Next to Carmen, the straitlaced Joe seems weak-willed and petulant. She's way too much woman for him—plus, she gets all the best lines. As Joe speeds over rough terrain in his jeep, she leans back and drawls, "Accelerate me all you want. The harder I get bumped, the more of me bounces."

Though she lures him away from his sweetheart, Cindy Lou (Olga James), and wrecks his promising future, it's hard to place all the blame on Carmen when Joe falls for her hook, line, and sinker, hopping willingly aboard an express elevator to hell.

Inevitably, Carmen grows restless. But she doesn't leave Joe without a reason; she runs because he tries to own her. She warns him she won't be chained from the get-go in her introductory number "Dat's Love": "If I chase you then you'll get caught / But once I got you I go my way!"

In song, Carmen makes it clear that she wants Joe because he's "hard to get" and that as soon as she's finished rocking his world, she'll leave him flat. In other words, she behaves as men have been allowed to for centuries. Tragically, Carmen must pay for her independence with her life.

After *Carmen Jones,* Dorothy Dandridge

was poised on the brink of superstardom. She shattered barriers as the first woman of color to be nominated for a Best Actress Oscar and the first to be featured on the cover of *Life* magazine. Sadly, her old anxieties took hold, and she clung to Preminger, who took complete control of

Dorothy Dandridge and Harry Belafonte

her life and career. As he forced her to refuse roles, her fame dwindled. Though the actress continued to make waves in *Island in the Sun* (1957) and *Porgy and Bess* (1959), mainstream acceptance in an unenlightened era eluded her. She died in 1965 at age forty-two.

In 1999, a new generation discovered this dynamic dame thanks to *Introducing Dorothy Dandridge*, a cable-TV biopic directed by Martha Coolidge. In her Golden Globe acceptance speech for Best Actress, Halle Berry tearfully told the crowd, "As you honor me, who you really honor is the eminent Dorothy Dandridge. She never got to stand here and be recognized by her peers, but because she lived, I am able to." In 2002, when Berry became the first African American woman to win an Academy Award for Best Actress for her role in *Monster's Ball*, she again acknowledged her predecessor. "This moment," she said, "belongs to Dorothy Dandridge."

Did You Know?

The original stage version of *Carmen Jones* was sung in a jazz style, for which Dandridge's own voice would have been ideal. But because Preminger insisted on vocals that recalled Bizet's *Carmen,* her singing voice was dubbed by opera diva Marilyn Horne.

Left to right: Nicodemus Stewart, Diahann Carroll, Dorothy Dandridge, Joe Adams, DeForest Covan, Pearl Bailey, and Roy Glenn

Marlene Dietrich

AS "CHRISTINE VOLE"

Witness for the Prosecution (1958)

Billy Wilder's *Witness for the Prosecution* gave the legendary
Marlene Dietrich a role she could really sink her teeth into—two roles, in fact. As Christine Vole, she's a clever German actress and adoring wife of the accused murderer Leonard Vole (Tyrone Power). As a nameless Cockney woman who sells damning evidence against Christine to Leonard's defense attorney, Sir Wilfrid Robards (Charles Laughton), she outsmarts everybody: the judge, the jury, the brilliant Sir Wilfrid, and especially her husband. The whole movie hinges on Dietrich's character; she is the titular witness for the prosecution. Perhaps only a handful of other film actresses in history could have pulled off this sneaky dual role as well as she does (Meryl Streep comes to mind).

From her Hollywood debut in Josef von Sternberg's *Morocco* (1930)—in which she famously performs a nightclub act tuxedo-clad and kisses a woman on the lips—to her often-emulated "Shanghai Lily" character in 1932's *Shanghai Express,* to her comic comeback in the western *Destry Rides Again* (1939), Dietrich became synonymous with sultry, world-weary Teutonic glamour. She also became the world's highest-paid entertainer by pushing the boundaries of gender roles. Gaining fame in the racy pre-Code era, she was shockingly open for her day, carrying on affairs with dozens of male and female costars, often traveling with both her husband and her lover(s).

The former Marie Magdalene Dietrich had survived the heady world of 1920s Berlin cabaret and was a veteran of fifty movies when she portrayed Christine Vole, a part she was determined to win. She was also dead set on working with Billy Wilder, who had directed her in *A Foreign Affair* in 1948. She brought the property to Wilder, telling him, "I'll only play the part if you direct," an offer he couldn't refuse. With her sculpted cheekbones and bedroom eyes, Marlene Dietrich, in his words, had "one of the greatest faces in the history of film."

And she fought to hold on to her beauty. Late in the film, Mr. Vole's girlfriend on the side sneers that Christine is "years older than he is." Actually, though she was nearly thirteen years his senior, Dietrich

Marlene Dietrich as Christine Vole and Charles Laughton as Wilfrid Robarts in *Witness for the Prosecution* looked fabulous compared to the handsome but weathered Power, who would die of a heart attack at age forty-four a mere three months after shooting on *Witness for the Prosecution* wrapped.

———◇———

> "What a wicked woman I am, and how brilliantly you exposed me and saved Leonard's life. The great Sir Wilfrid Robarts did it again. Well, let me tell you something. You didn't do it alone. You had help."
>
> —"CHRISTINE VOLE"

———◇———

Witness for the Prosecution boasts Dietrich at her most empowered. Seemingly, Laughton is the film's hero as the respected barrister "Wilfrid the Fox." But he's ultimately tripped up by what one could argue is a kind of male-chauvinist thinking. Preparing to meet the wife of his client, Wilfrid speculates that she may need smelling salts when she becomes hysterical and faints. He is thunderstruck when in strolls Christine, a paragon of composure. "I do not think that will be necessary," she informs him. "I never faint, because I'm not sure that I will fall gracefully." He suspects she's up to something, but—perhaps because she's

a woman—he seems to underestimate her ability to pull the wool so completely over his eyes. In the final scene, she casually touches up her lipstick in the courtroom while explaining how she's triple-crossed him. She then goes full gangsta by delivering the final whiplash-inducing twist in the story, violently bringing events to their logical, if unpredictable, conclusion. Searching for words, Sir Wilfrid merely repeats his earlier assessment of Christine: "What a remarkable woman." Not only has this remarkable woman just played him for a sucker, but she's also taken justice into her own hands, succeeding where the legal system failed.

This strong female character was made possible by a woman who remains, over forty years after her death, the world's

Christine Vole testifies.

Dietrich shows off her famous legs as she chats with a reporter on set.

best-selling novelist of all time. Only the Bible and the plays of Shakespeare have been read more than the detective fiction of Agatha Christie, who penned the suspenseful short story *Traitor's Hands* in 1925. In 1948, it was retitled *Witness for the Prosecution,* and it was adapted into a play in 1953. Years after Billy Wilder turned it into a popular movie, he credited Christie's finely tuned plot with its success. "Agatha Christie constructed like an angel, full of surprises," he said. "For every five hundred great dialogue writers, there are five great constructionists. That's the toughest job in the world."

Did You Know?

Acclaimed playwright Noël Coward coached Marlene Dietrich on her Cockney accent. In his diary, Coward recalled, "It is not easy to teach Cockney to a German glamour-puss who can't pronounce her Rs, but she did astonishingly well."

Pam Grier

AS "MS. COFFIN, A.K.A. 'COFFY'"

Coffy (1973)

Coffy is one bad mutha. By day a respected operating-room nurse, at night she takes the law into her own hands to exact revenge on the drug pushers who got her kid sister hooked on smack. Coffy hides weapons in her afro, swears like a sailor, and, as the *Los Angeles Times* noted in its 1973 review, "has a bullet destined for the crotch or the head, or a sharpened bobby pin aimed at the jugular vein of every white Mafioso in sight." This chick is not to be trifled with.

"Only Pam Grier could have made it work," writer/director Jack Hill has said of *Coffy*. Hill wrote the titular role in his first *blaxploitation* outing for Grier, a young actress he had directed in two women-behind-bars pictures, *The Big Doll House* (1971) and *The Big Bird Cage* (1972). But *Coffy* was something completely different: a movie with a powerful African American woman as its heroine. Not just any heroine, but a one-woman vigilante force who never submits, never apologizes, and walks away unpunished in the end. It made Pam Grier an enormous cult star.

Raised to be tough and self-sufficient by her military father and nurse mother, Grier learned acting on the job, carrying a copy of Konstantin Stanislavski's *An Actor Prepares* with her everywhere. "My role in *Coffy* reminded me of my mother, a nurse

who stood up for herself," she recalled. This nurse stands up for herself with a vengeance. After blowing the head off of one dope pusher, she turns to his henchman. "It was easy for him because he really didn't believe it was comin'," she says, "but it ain't gonna be easy for you, because you better believe it's comin'!" She's not above standing up to women who try to push her around, either, dumping a bowl of salad on a belligerent hooker before slicing up her hands with the razor blades concealed in her coiffure.

When she burst on the scene in *Coffy*, Pam Grier ignited a new trend in blax-ploitation films, one that reflected the women's lib movement of the early 1970s. "Women were demanding equal rights to men," Grier wrote in her 2010 autobi-ography, *Foxy*. "It's as if we walked out of the kitchen, took off our aprons, put

FATAL FEMMES

Pam Grier as Ms. Coffin in *Coffy*

"So you wanna play with knives, huh? Well, you picked the wrong player!"

—"COFFY"

on our platform shoes, bell bottoms, and halter tops, and we were ready to play like men—and with men." More often than not, women in seventies exploitation films were scantily clad victims. Not Ms. Grier. Coffy may undress, but her nudity never victimizes her. On the contrary, her body—like the sawed-off shotgun she packs—is a weapon she wields to take down lowlife pushers and pimps.

The concept for *Coffy* originated with American International Pictures' head of production, Larry Gordon, who hired Jack Hill to direct what he called a "black woman revenge film." Though it was shot in eighteen days on a skimpy $500,000 budget, Hill fought to squeeze more quality and more social conscience into the project than studio execs thought it needed. Many of the bigwigs in charge, Hill recalled in 2001, "had nothing but contempt for the material they were working with, contempt for the audience it was made for." But he insisted on treating the material—and its star—with a little R-E-S-P-E-C-T.

It was initially intended only for drive-

Writer/director Jack Hill and Pam Grier on set

ins, but *Coffy* turned out so exceptional that it was distributed to major theaters across the country. In the wake of its success, Grier and Hill reteamed for a follow-up, *Foxy Brown* (1974), another smash for AIP. This time around, the soundtrack is funkier, the bell bottoms bigger, and the action way over the top, including a scene where Foxy douses a skinhead in gasoline and lights him on fire. Its star later revealed that she and her ballsy character were in perfect sync. "Foxy Brown was a fighter," she said, "and so was I."

In 1997, edgy auteur Quentin Tarantino tailored a script specifically for Pam Grier. "It's my version of *Foxy Brown*," he told her. In tribute, Tarantino titled his film *Jackie Brown*. With the likes of Robert De Niro, Michael Keaton, Samuel L. Jackson, and Bridget Fonda supporting her, the star of *Coffy* had finally hit the big time.

Did You Know?

In 1975, Pam Grier became the first woman of color to appear on the cover of Gloria Steinem's *Ms.* magazine.

Left: Pam Grier is locked and loaded as Coffy. Right: Pam Grier, Leslie McRae (in purple dress), and a bevy of background talent on the set of *Coffy*

Ladies Who Laugh

Laughter goes a long way. In life or in the movies, a woman who makes us laugh can get away with more—more toughness, more frankness, more determination. The following comedy queens manage to be strong and self-assured, as well as witty. Using a giggle and a wink instead of a battering ram, they accomplish great things.

Rosalind Russell

AS "HILDY JOHNSON"

His Girl Friday (1940)

As Hildy Johnson in Howard Hawks's screwball comedy *His Girl Friday,* Rosalind Russell is the ultimate fast-talking dame and the quintessential career woman. Though she's the titular character, the film's title is a misnomer; Hildy is nobody's girl Friday—she's a star reporter in her own right.

By the time she played Hildy, Connecticut-born Russell had been in Hollywood for several years, filling mainly supporting roles in starched dramas. She fought to play the catty Sylvia Fowler in George Cukor's comedy *The Women* (1939), and once it was released, her jaw-droppingly loony performance transformed her image and career overnight. Suddenly, she was one of the screen's great comediennes. When Ginger Rogers, Claudette Colbert, Irene Dunne, Jean Arthur, and Carole Lombard all turned down the female lead opposite Cary Grant in *His Girl Friday,* Columbia arranged to borrow Russell from MGM at the last minute. It must have been fate, because it's now virtually impossible to imagine any other actress in the role.

Hawks encouraged his actors to draw from their personalities to improvise their own bits and gags. He also had them talk at breakneck speed—around 240 words per minute (as opposed to the average rate of 100 to 150). Early in the production, Russell began to feel that Hawks was giving all the funniest dialogue to Grant, so she hired an ad writer to create some additional comedic lines for her. "We went wild," Russell recalled, "overlapped our dialogue, waited for no man. And Hawks loved it." Soon, her character became the dominant force of the picture.

Though Grant is uproariously snide as her editor and ex-husband, Walter Burns, *His Girl Friday* is really Hildy's movie. In the opening scene, the camera follows her as she enters the newsroom, all decked out in a smart pinstriped suit and mini stovepipe hat, a fashionista with fierce comic timing. As Jeanine Basinger observes in her book *A Woman's View,* Russell "never looks anything but handsome and well dressed, but—something she shares with Lucille Ball—she can be both elegant *and* ridiculous, holding the two qualities together in a single performance."

Rosalind Russell as Hildy Johnson in *His Girl Friday*

Cary Grant and Rosalind Russell

Hildy can write circles around her male colleagues, but she thinks she wants to quit, marry her stodgy fiancé, Bruce (Ralph Bellamy), and become a full-time housewife. "I'm going to be a woman, not a news-getting machine," she frequently threatens. "I'm going to have babies and take care of them and give them cod liver oil and watch their teeth grow." Who is she kidding? Maybe she repeats it so often to convince herself. We, of course, know she would be miserable baking pies and changing diapers, as do her coworkers, who wager that her marriage won't last six months. It's obvious to everyone except Hildy that she's a born "newspaper man."

When a disturbed criminal escapes, she rushes to the scene of the jailbreak, sprinting through dark Manhattan streets

> "Hear that? That's the story I just wrote. Yes, yes, I know we had a bargain. I just said I'd write it, I didn't say I wouldn't tear it up. It's all in little pieces now, Walter. And I hope to do the same for you someday!"
>
> —"HILDY JOHNSON"

in her high heels and hiked-up pencil skirt. Russell's crowning glory of physical comedy comes when she chases down the prison warden to bribe a story out of him. She tackles the stocky man like a defensive linebacker, throwing her body on top of his and clinching him in a wrestling hold so he can't get away.

Cary Grant, Rosalind Russell, and Howard Hawks on set

Finally, she accepts that her place is in the newsroom with Walter, not at home with Bruce. "I'm no suburban bridge player," she declares in a journalistic frenzy, writing a story that will save a man's life. "I'm a newspaper man!" As they exit the final frame, Walter lets Hildy struggle to carry her heavy suitcase down a flight of stairs. In his own caustic way, he shows his respect for her by treating her like he would a man—like an equal—rather than coddling her within an inch of her life, as Bruce does.

For *His Girl Friday,* Roz raked in glowing reviews. Henceforth, she became Hollywood's go-to career-driven lady. "I played— I think it was twenty-three career women," she later said. "I've been every kind of executive and I've owned everything— factories and advertising agencies and pharmaceutical houses." Of all those working women, the actress always considered Hildy her favorite.

As she matured, Russell branched out in unexpected directions, forming a production company in 1948 with her husband (agent Frederick Brisson), winning a Tony award for the stage musical *Wonderful Town* in 1953, and embodying the role of Auntie Mame on both stage and screen.

Did You Know?

Russell coscripted *The Unguarded Moment,* a 1956 film starring Esther Williams as a teacher who is sexually harassed at work. Along with Ida Lupino, Russell was one of a few in the industry confronting the topic of sexual harassment.

Katharine Hepburn

AS "AMANDA BONNER"

Adam's Rib (1949)

Katharine Hepburn made a lengthy career out of playing
dynamic dames. Though she portrayed a wide range of types over the course of sixty-four years, most of her characters seem driven by a fundamental feminism, a quest for male-female equality that was either voiced aloud or silently implied. In her early days, she practically cornered the market on the independent, intelligent modern woman; *Little Women* (1933), *Sylvia Scarlett* (1936), *A Woman Rebels* (1936), and *Dragon Seed* (1944) are examples of Kate at her most assertive. "Different from any woman I've ever known," is how Herbert Marshall's character describes her Victorian proto-feminist Pamela in *A Woman Rebels*. "Nothing helpless about you." Pamela calmly replies, "Don't you think that 'dependent' myth about women is one that men created for their own protection?" The viewpoints she expressed in these films are still relevant today.

Hepburn's screen persona was no act. Raised by a suffragette mother and liberal father to be intellectually progressive, she rebelled by wearing pants when few women dared, having unmarried relationships with men, and choosing not to have children. By doing things her own way, she became a Hollywood power player. "She usually got anything she wanted," *Adam's Rib* co-screenwriter Garson Kanin said, "because she would show up wearing the traditional slacks, and she'd barge in to their offices and give 'em hell." When

Kate used her hard-won clout at MGM to demand Spencer Tracy as her costar in *Woman of the Year* (1942), she finally met her match, both on and off the screen. A legendary chemistry was sparked, and a classic movie pairing was born.

In 1949's *Adam's Rib*, they are married lawyers Adam and Amanda Bonner. Like Pamela in *A Woman Rebels*, Amanda is an outspoken feminist—but this time, it's played for laughs. She crusades for equal rights to the point that it threatens her otherwise happy marriage. "There are lots of

Katharine Hepburn as Amanda Bonner in *Adam's Rib*

"There's no room in marriage
for what used to be known as 'the little woman.'
She's got to be as big as the man is."
—"AMANDA BONNER"

things that a man can do, and in society's eyes it's all hunky-dory," she explains to Adam. "A woman does the same thing—the same, mind you—and she's an outcast." At first, he humors her: "You sound cute when you get cause-y." When she defends Doris Attinger (Judy Holliday), a woman who shot her philandering, abusive husband (Tom Ewell)—who happens to be represented by Adam—the Bonners' relationship is strained to the breaking point.

The clever, wildly funny, and sophisticated script was written by the husband-and-wife team of Kanin and Ruth Gordon, close friends of Tracy and Hepburn. Kanin and Gordon observed the way the two stars bantered in their private lives and copied that dynamic for the film. The Bonners share inside jokes, debate ideas together, and treat each other with mutual respect. When Amanda breaks down bawling over the "typical instinctive masculine brutality" of Adam's playful spank on her behind, he accuses her of trying that old "guaranteed heart-melter: a few female tears." She dries her eyes, regains her composure, and kicks him in the shin—hard. Now it gets physical.

Supported by two hilarious ladies, Jean Hagen (in her film debut) and Judy Holliday (who would deliver an Oscar-winning

performance in *Born Yesterday* the following year), Hepburn's Amanda attempts to prove in court "that woman is the equal of man." At home, she and Adam volley their battle-of-the-sexes opinions back and forth through the entire film. Each chalks up victories and defeats—she makes him look foolish and wins the case, he succeeds in exposing her hypocrisy—and they finally reach a draw in the end. They agree that men and women are different, but equal, which is exactly what Amanda got carried away trying to prove in the first place.

Tracy, Hepburn, and director George Cukor on set

Katharine Hepburn and Spencer Tracy

As the 1940s gave way to the fifties—and much of the independence women had gained during the war was lost as they were expected to conform to more traditional roles—many formerly empowered actresses were cast as embittered viragos or victims. Barbara Stanwyck went from Fred MacMurray's seductive manipulator in *Double Indemnity* (1944) to Burt Lancaster's nagging, plotted-against wife in *Sorry, Wrong Number* (1948); Gene Tierney went from cunning controller in *Leave Her to Heaven* (1945) to fragile, brainwashed pawn in *Whirlpool* (1949). But the Great Kate never took roles that robbed her of her dignity. She garnered acclaim playing strong-willed spinster Rosie (opposite Humphrey Bogart) in *The African Queen* (1951) and the delicate Jane in *Summertime* (1955), among other memorable roles. In

1967, she teamed with Tracy for one final go-round in *Guess Who's Coming to Dinner*, a groundbreaking comedy about interracial marriage costarring Sidney Poitier and Hepburn's niece and namesake, Katharine Houghton. The performance won Hepburn the second of a record four Academy Awards for Best Actress.

Did You Know?

Katharine Hepburn conspired with the screenwriters and director George Cukor to showcase Judy Holliday's talent in the film. When Amanda first meets with Mrs. Attinger, Hepburn keeps her face turned away from the camera and lets Holliday steal all the attention. Cukor shot the five-minute scene without a single cut.

Julie Andrews
AS "MARY POPPINS"

Mary Poppins (1964)

She follows nobody's rules except her own. She refuses to

explain anything, even when her employer demands it. She shows no respect for the patriarchal establishment. And she never permits sentiment to muddle her thinking. No, I'm not talking about Pam Grier in *Foxy Brown*. I'm talking about Mary Poppins, the woman who can do it all, from sliding up the banister to commanding inanimate objects at her will. She's magical, she's wonderful, and she's powerful.

Poppins sprang from the active imagination of Australian-born Helen Goff, who relocated to London and renamed herself Pamela Travers at age twenty-five. She published the first in a series of books about the extraordinary English nanny under the pen name of P.L. Travers in 1934. Thirty years later, with the reluctant assistance of Travers (who feared her character would be ruined), Walt Disney created a colorful, feel-good musical with original songs by Richard and Robert Sherman and a genuinely witty script by Bill Walsh. Perhaps unintentionally, *Mary Poppins* turned out to be one of the most subversive feminist films of the 1960s, a feat all the more impressive because it's cloaked in the guise of candy-coated family fare.

George Banks (David Tomlinson) believes himself to be "the lord of my cas-tle" and treats his "subjects, servants, children, wife, with a firm but gentle hand." Behind his back, Mrs. Banks (Glynis Johns) is a hardcore suffragette, throwing rotten eggs at the prime minister and marching for women's votes. Their children, Jane and Michael, suffer from a lack of parental involvement.

In flies Mary Poppins—Julie Andrews in her knockout film debut—who completely dominates Mr. Banks. Turning the tables on the hiring process, *she* interviews *him*. "I make it a point never to give references," she informs him, and promptly hires herself for the job. Though she's the children's nanny, she's not self-sacrificing or humble, as maternal types are expected to be; she has an ego. It's immodest for an Edwardian lady to describe herself as "practically perfect in every way," to enjoy

Julie Andrews as Mary Poppins in *Mary Poppins*

looking at herself in a mirror, and to win a merry-go-round horserace, but she doesn't care. "She's very vain, you know," observed Andrews, who won an Oscar for perfectly portraying Mary.

"I should like to make one thing quite clear. . . . I never explain anything."

—"MARY POPPINS"

Nobody messes with Poppins. Much like Travers, she's a prickly perfectionist and something of a control freak. Yet she brings enchantment to the most mundane chores, making every day a jolly holiday for her steady date Bert (Dick Van Dyke). Floating down from a cloud to transform the Bankses' lives, she is practically an all-powerful superhuman—almost a goddess. Though Disney and Travers never quite saw eye to eye, the two joined forces to create an unforgettable movie character, a proper British firebrand who shifts the power structure in a male-dominated household.

She not only manipulates George into taking the children to the bank (and makes him believe he thought of it himself as "just the medicine they need for all this slipshod, sugary female thinking they get around here all day"), but she also plants the seeds of revolt in Michael's head with her song "Feed the Birds," very nearly inciting anarchy! Finally, when his world is turned upside down by Mary, George learns that being a father is not about bossing his family around, but about being a friend to them.

In the last scene, Mrs. Banks lets her feminist flag fly, attaching a "Votes for Women" banner to the tail of a kite. This serves a dual purpose, signaling that she will be a more attentive mother and showing the world that she supports women's rights. "One of the things that *Poppins* is about—and nobody really realizes it—is women's liberation," Robert Sherman has said. "Though Mrs. Banks may not be the perfect women's libber, Mary Poppins certainly was. She's both very feminine, and very much in control at the same time."

Since the 1964 film, Mary has become a cultural icon, having been revamped as a stage musical in 2004 and popping back into movie theaters (with Emily Blunt in the title role) in 2018's *Mary Poppins Returns*. The behind-the-scenes story of Disney and Travers was illuminated in the 2013 movie *Saving Mr. Banks*.

Did You Know?

Walt Disney first approached Pamela Travers about selling the film rights to her Mary Poppins books in 1944. He persisted for nineteen years, finally getting her to sign over the rights in 1963.

Julie Andrews and Walt Disney have tea on the soundstage.

Glynis Johns as Mrs. Banks

Dick Van Dyke, Karen Dotrice, Matthew Garber, and Julie Andrews on the rooftops of London

Jane Fonda

AS "CAT BALLOU"

Cat Ballou (1965)

The western has a long-held tradition of sidelining women.

The real Annie Oakley was a spitfire who could outshoot any man, but in *Annie Oakley* (1935) and *Annie Get Your Gun* (1950), Hollywood turned her into a lovesick glamour girl, as they did for Belle Starr in the 1941 film starring Gene Tierney. Doris Day later suffered a similar fate in *Calamity Jane* (1953). Before Jane Fonda hopped on a horse in *Cat Ballou*, tough female gunslingers were a cinematic anomaly best exemplified by Barbara Stanwyck in *The Furies* (1950) and *Forty Guns* (1957) and Joan Crawford in *Johnny Guitar* (1954). Then, along came Cat, leading her own gang of male outlaws and doing it all in the name of comedy. It was the movie that took Fonda from ingénue to leading lady.

The project started with Roy Chanslor's 1956 novel *The Ballad of Cat Ballou*, a straightforward western tale in which Cat is not the hero, but the hormonal teenage daughter of the main characters. In 1964, producer Harold Hecht and screenwriter Frank R. Pierson had the idea to transform the story into a western satire, with Cat as the central character. Jane Fonda had little interest in it, but, at the suggestion of her fiancé, director Roger Vadim, she took the role. She admirably plays it straight with a cast of zany wild-west characters buzzing around her.

Heralded by a Greek chorus of two banjo-pickin' troubadours, played by Stubby Kaye and Nat King Cole (in his final appearance before his untimely death at age forty-five), Cat goes from innocent school teacher to revenge-crazed outlaw when a crooked Wyoming land developer has her father killed. She is literally told "Don't you worry your pretty little head about it" by the sheriff. What self-respecting female could let that one slide? She rounds up a posse of cowardly gunmen and the notorious drunken gunfighter Kid Shelleen (Lee Marvin), but the men do nothing until she spurs them into action. When they object to her suggestion of robbing a train, Cat explodes: "If people didn't try something new, there wouldn't hardly be any progress at all!"

Soon, she and her gang are in over their heads. Her beau, Clay (Michael Callan), offers to marry Cat and take her away to

Jane Fonda as Cat Ballou in *Cat Ballou*

Michael Callan, Tom Nardini, and Dwayne Hickman look on as Cat reacts to the death of her father, played by John Marley.

St. Louis, but she is outraged at the idea. "Of all the self-centered and egotistical things I ever heard! Why do men always think that marriage is the only thing that women have on their minds?" She doesn't want marriage; she wants love, respect, and revenge. But mostly revenge.

While the guys are busy brawling among themselves, our heroine takes matters into her own hands, masquerading as a saloon girl named Trixie and threatening the town's villainous head honcho Sir Harry Percival (Reginald Denny) with a concealed pistol. Because she's a cute young thing, he makes the fatal mistake of underestimating her. His final words are: "I don't think you have it in you, Miss Ballou. Give me that gun." He learns the hard way that she has it in her, after all.

When Cat is captured and arrested, angry villagers shout "Jezebel!" as she walks to the noose to be hanged. Haters gonna hate, but this whimsical western has a happy ending. In the nick of time, her gang stages a daring rescue, and she rides off into the sunset to become a legend. The troubadours hail her as "Queen of the Outlaws, Her Highness Cat Ballou."

Cat Ballou has a distinct feminist tone that was unusual for 1965; it even pre-dates Jane Fonda's activism. After the film won critical praise and an Oscar for Lee Marvin, Jane's career caught fire. She married

"You'll never make me cry!"

—"CAT BALLOU"

and divorced Vadim and became a powerful force in Hollywood, winning her own Oscars for *Klute* (1971) and for a movie she conceived and produced herself, *Coming Home*, a 1978 drama about a disabled Vietnam War veteran. It was in the 1970s that she began to champion the cause of women's rights. "Feminism is not just about women," she has said. "It's about letting all people lead fuller lives."

By the 1980s, Fonda had acquired the prestige to shepherd her own projects, including the female-driven comedy *9 to 5*

(1980) and the fitness empire she built with *Jane Fonda's Workout* in 1981. Long after her so-called retirement in the 1990s, Fonda remains a working actress and iconic woman.

Did You Know?

Jane Fonda credited Lee Marvin for teaching her to stand up for herself professionally. When she consented to retake after retake on the set of *Cat Ballou*, Marvin took her aside and advised, "You have to get some backbone, girl. Learn to say no when they ask you to keep working."

Henry Fonda visits his daughter on the set of *Cat Ballou*.

Goldie Hawn

AS "JUDY BENJAMIN"

Private Benjamin (1980)

Before Judy Benjamin joins the army, she caters to the men in her life. When she's not busy spending their money, she lights her father's cigars and submits to the sexual demands of her self-absorbed husband. Her greatest conflict is with the upholsterer, who presents her with an ottoman trimmed in beige material instead of mushroom. "I'm sure you could have found a little mushroom fabric—a yard," she whimpers.

Then she becomes Private Benjamin.

Over the course of basic training, Judy learns to stand up for herself, transforming from "whiny candy-ass" (as one of her fellow privates describes her) to strong-willed soldier—kicking, screaming, and chipping her nail polish the whole way. Surviving barbed wire, land mines, sexual harassment, and her vindictive leader, Captain Lewis (played to repugnant perfection by Eileen Brennan), Private Benjamin navigates a collision course from dominated to dominant. The army makes an independent woman out of her.

At first glance a funny fish-out-of-water story, *Private Benjamin* is actually a movie about a person developing a strong sense of self and rising to meet her full potential. The first half of the film is a loose remake of the 1953 Rosalind Russell vehicle *Never Wave at a WAC*; the second half branches off into new territory. When she's trans-ferred to Paris and faced with the temptation to marry a sexy French doctor (Armand Assante) who treats her little better than he does his dog, Judy decides she's better off on her own. By the final frame, she's 180 degrees from where she began.

Behind the scenes, the film was a labor of love for leading-lady-turned-producer Goldie Hawn and cowriter/producer Nancy Meyers. Along with cowriters and producers Charles Shyer and Harvey Miller and director Howard Zieff, the two women crafted what Hawn referred to as "a dream role for any actress. There was no male star to carry the picture....The female lead carries the whole movie, almost by herself." Like her newborn daughter, Kate Hudson, whom she nursed right on set, *Private Benjamin* received Goldie's hands-on nurturing. She oversaw every aspect of the production while managing to deliver an Oscar-nominated comic

Goldie Hawn as Judy Benjamin in *Private Benjamin*

Private Benjamin is the only female member of the elite Thornbirds squadron.

performance that in 2000 was ranked eighty-second on the American Film Institute's list of America's 100 Funniest Movies and served as Reese Witherspoon's inspiration as she produced and starred in the 2001 comedy *Legally Blonde.*

But it wasn't easy to get the feminist film off the ground. After Nancy Meyers made it to the top of the ladder as "the most successful female director in Hollywood" (according to *The Independent* magazine in 2010)—helming *What Women Want* (2000), *Something's Gotta Give* (2003), and *It's Complicated* (2009), among others—she recalled the difficulty she had faced in 1979. Though Goldie Hawn was a big name, having found fame as a ditzy blonde in the 1960s TV series *Laugh-In* and winning an Oscar for the 1969 comedy

Cactus Flower, her involvement did not guarantee a green light. "*Private Benjamin* got turned down by every studio until the very last one," Meyers said. "At the end of the movie, she hits the groom in the face and then walks away from the wedding. People didn't want to see [Hawn] in that part. In fact, one studio executive told her the film was a career ender. There was real resistance to it on a deeper level than just they didn't like this script."

Warner Bros. finally gave the project a go, and the rest is history. Hawn was thrilled with *Private Benjamin*'s box-office success, but felt the sting later. Once she was a star/producer, certain studio execs attached a stigma to her, assuming she was bossy or demanding, making it harder for her to get cast as an actress. "The

> ## "I did join the army, but I joined a *different* army. I joined the one with the condos and the private rooms."
> —"JUDY BENJAMIN"

double-edged sword of my supposed new power in Hollywood," she lamented, "stuck in my side." She later regretted her decision not to produce *Swing Shift* (1984), finding herself powerless to intervene when the story she had envisioned veered in the wrong direction. Hawn saw her original intention—to make a statement about working women during World War II and how their power was taken away when the soldiers returned—become watered down until the message was largely lost.

But Goldie walked away from *Swing Shift* with a consolation prize: her costar, Kurt Russell. The two quickly became a Hollywood power couple and have lived happily together ever since. In 1987, they starred together in *Overboard*, a romantic comedy executive-produced by Hawn.

Did You Know?

In her 2005 memoir, *A Lotus Grows in the Mud*, Goldie Hawn described costar Eileen Brennan as her "comedic soul mate." She wrote, "Eileen and I are on the same wavelength, hearing the same music that connects our timing without words or need for translation."

Eileen Brennan, Hal Williams, and Goldie Hawn

Melanie Griffith

AS "TESS McGILL"

Working Girl (1988)

"Power to the people," Harrison Ford toasts before gulping his tequila in *Working Girl.* "The little people," adds Melanie Griffith in a voice so quiet that only the audience can hear her. It's a small but telling line in Mike Nichols's 1988 ode to little people with big dreams. And no one dreams bigger than Griffith's Tess, an ambitious secretary who—in a mere two weeks—metamorphoses from tacky Staten Island working girl to upwardly mobile Manhattan sophisticate while her insufferable boss recovers from a skiing accident.

Sure, Tess kicks aside a few rules in the process, but, as she reminds us, "If you're someone like me, you can't get there without bending the rules." Besides, the boss lady has it coming. Sigourney Weaver turns in a brilliant comic performance as Katherine Parker, a privileged barracuda ("I'd love to help you, but you can't busy the quarterback with passing out the Gatorade.") who gets whatever she wants, even if it means stealing ideas from her employees.

Though some have criticized the film for portraying female bosses in a negative light, screenwriter Kevin Wade never intended to imply that all powerful women are conniving. Griffith and Weaver, he said, play "two modern women who are forced by the system into using traditional combat techniques." As nasty as Katherine is, the real villain is the system.

This underdog comedy-drama is loaded with feminine talent. Supporting Griffith and Weaver are Joan Cusack (whose power hair is teased out bigger than her power shoulder pads), Olympia Dukakis, *Saturday Night Live*'s Nora Dunn, and, in a brief cameo, Ricki Lake. Mega-singer/songwriter Carly Simon adds her voice to the mix, belting her way to an Oscar on the film's soundtrack. The male talent is pretty impressive, too: Harrison Ford as the mutual love interest of both leading ladies, a hilariously unctuous Alec Baldwin, and a pre-fame (and pre-scandal) Kevin Spacey in a bit part.

But it's Tess McGill's movie all the way. With its razor-sharp script by first-time screenwriter Wade and impeccable direction by the seasoned Nichols, *Working Girl* is a rarity: a great mainstream film

LADIES WHO LAUGH

Melanie Griffith as Tess McGill in *Working Girl*

> ### "I'm not gonna spend the rest of my life working my ass off and getting nowhere just because I followed rules that I had nothing to do with setting up."
>
> —"TESS McGILL"

that follows a female lead as she fights class discrimination, gender bias, sexual harassment, and cutthroat colleagues to make it to the top in the business world. The secretary-makes-good theme hadn't been explored so successfully since the days when spunky gals like Jean Arthur bluffed their way from lowly stenographers to big shots in 1930s screwball comedies (see *More Than a Secretary* [1936] and *Easy Living* [1937]). Here, this working girl is free to be both smart and unabashedly sexy. "I have a head for business," Tess purrs, "and a bod for sin."

Mirroring the on-screen Cinderella story was Melanie Griffith's behind-the-scenes struggle to land the lead role. Though she is the daughter of Hitchcock blonde Tippi Hedren, Griffith did not have an easy climb to acting success. "I wanted to do *Working Girl* for a year and a half before Mike Nichols was attached," she told the *Los Angeles Times* in 1988, "but they [the studio] didn't think I was a big enough star." When Nichols came on board, he fought for her, telling the studio he would not direct the movie unless Melanie Griffith played Tess. It was a star-making performance for the

actress. Critics compared her comic style to that of Judy Holliday and her charisma to that of Jean Harlow and Marilyn Monroe.

The movie was a box-office smash. It was even up for a Best Picture Oscar, an uncommon achievement for a comedy. Griffith was nominated for Best Actress, with both Weaver and Cusack earning Supporting Actress nominations.

In the current climate of greater awareness about women's empowerment, it's time to rediscover *Working Girl* as a celebration of ambitious women who refuse to lie down and let this so-called man's world steamroll over them. Tess has the brains, the ingenuity, and the drive; why shouldn't she get the money, the acclaim, and the corner office that her male counterparts snag while she's busy pouring their coffee? In the words of Tess, "damn straight."

Did You Know?

Four different Manhattan buildings were used for the interiors of the Petty-Marsh offices where Tess and Katherine work, including one of the World Trade Center towers that was destroyed in the 9/11 attacks in 2001.

I DYNAMIC DAMES

Top: Melanie Griffith and Joan Cusack. Bottom: Sigourney Weaver, Harrison Ford, and Melanie Griffith

Women of Mystery

They don't scare easy. They don't cower in the corner
and wait for a man to save them. They never run away from
things that go bump in the night; they stick around and investigate.
Whether they're female sleuths, amateur detectives, or average
women who find themselves entangled in nefarious goings-on, these
characters are comfortable mingling with the mysterious.

Myrna Loy

AS "NORA CHARLES"

The Thin Man (1934)

Myrna Loy had appeared in more than eighty movies before landing the role that would make her a household name. As the quick-witted wife of ex-gumshoe Nick Charles (William Powell) in *The Thin Man,* she is suave, stylish, and capable of dishing her husband's sarcastic remarks right back at him, matching him insult for insult and drink for drink. She also financially supports him (and their wire-haired terrier, Asta) with her inherited money. As Loy observed in her 1987 autobiography, "*The Thin Man* virtually introduced modern marriage to the screen."

Together, Loy and Powell pioneered a form of comic elegance by breezily underplaying their jokes. Back then, comedy was new territory for Loy. Though her acerbic wit was displayed in 1932's *Love Me Tonight* (when asked "Do you ever think of anything but men?" her character replies, "Yes. Schoolboys."), that was an atypical part. "I'd fired an occasional quip, but my roles had been very straight up to that point," she recalled. Her boss at MGM, Louis B. Mayer, saw no reason for Myrna to deviate from straight drama, and he fought director Woody Van Dyke over his lead actress of choice. "She's all right," Van Dyke told Mayer. "I've pushed her in my pool." Mayer finally consented, on the condition that they finish shooting in three weeks. They did better than that—*The Thin Man* was made in sixteen days.

Nora Charles has one of the most memorable comedic introductions in movie history. Toting a tower of Christmas presents and a dog on a leash, she trips and falls face-forward on a barroom floor, without a stunt double. "I must have been crazy. I could have killed myself," remembered Loy. "I dashed in with Asta and all those packages, tripped myself, went down, slid across the floor, and hit the mark with my chin. It was absolutely incredible!"

Nick and Nora have a fresh, playful sexuality between them that was missing from most fictional married couples at that time. When the police enter their bedroom and search Nora's dresser, she asks her husband, "What's that man doing in my drawers?" Nick spits out his scotch and gapes like a little boy at her unintentional double entendre. He also calls her "Shugah" and

Myrna Loy as Nora Charles in *The Thin Man*

"Go on, see if I care! But I think it's
a dirty trick to bring me all the way to
New York just to make a widow of me."

—"NORA CHARLES"

drunkenly admits he's a sucker for "lanky brunettes with wicked jaws." She, in turn, is thrilled by his detective work, forever urging him to do a little sleuthing.

Not only does this couple have fun with marriage, but they also have fun with murder—a virtually unprecedented double no-no that "scared the hell out of the whole studio," according to MGM story editor Samuel Marx. Neither murder nor matrimony was supposed to be treated so casually, but *The Thin Man* broke both of those traditions, thanks to Dashiell Hammett's hard-boiled yet lighthearted mystery novel that formed the basis of the film. Hammett's longtime lady friend, playwright Lillian Hellman, inspired the character of Nora.

The movie was a surprise hit with audiences and critics. *Screenland* magazine labeled Myrna "The New Sophisticate of the

William Powell, Skippy (as Asta), and Myrna Loy on set

Myrna Loy in a publicity portrait for *The Thin Man*

though the two were equally responsible for the film's success. "I wanted what Bill was getting, that's all," she has said. When the studio powers that be denied her request, the actress went on strike, refusing to work for nearly a year until Mayer agreed to her terms. "I fought him and nearly drove him crazy at times, but in spite of our battles, I always held my own and earned his respect," she wrote of Mayer. "I never had to play kneesies with him."

Once she received equal compensation, Loy reteamed with Powell for five *Thin Man* sequels. Hollywood, meanwhile, was attempting to recapture that Nick and Nora magic with similar husband-and-wife detective comedies: *Fast and Loose* (1939) with Robert Montgomery and Rosalind Russell, *Mr. and Mrs. North* (1942) with Gracie Allen and William Post Jr., and *Having Wonderful Crime* (1945) with Carole Landis and George Murphy were among the copycats.

Screen," while journalist Elizabeth Wilson gushed in 1934, "I have seen *The Thin Man* three times, but am quite sure that someday I shall just have to see Myrna with that ice bag on her head, and hear her say 'I was a gleam in my father's eye' just one more time."

Despite her popularity, MGM only paid Loy half of what William Powell earned,

Did You Know?

Though he played her screen husband for thirteen years, William Powell and Myrna Loy were never romantically involved. "Oh, there were times when Bill had a crush on me and times when I had a crush on Bill," she said, "but we never made anything of it. We worked around it and stayed pals."

Bonita Granville

AS "NANCY DREW"

Nancy Drew ... Detective (1938)

After the phenomenal success of *The Thin Man,* the comedy-mystery was all the rage in Hollywood. Starting in 1938, Warner Bros. unleashed a series of jaunty whodunits featuring a young female sleuth who had become wildly popular since her debut in the 1930 novel *The Secret of the Old Clock:* Nancy Drew.

The first movie, *Nancy Drew ... Detective,* loosely based on the 1933 book *The Password to Larkspur Lane,* introduced fifteen-year-old Bonita Granville as Nancy and established the formula the others would follow. Nancy sniffs out a crime, vows to solve it ("I'll show you—all of you!"), is told to "stay out of it" by her father, is thrown off track, manipulates her crush Ted (Frankie Thomas) into helping her investigate, is captured and locked in a basement, and finally brings the criminals to justice—all in sixty-six minutes flat. The brisk unfolding of the plots was rivaled only by the speed at which the movies were churned out: four in less than one year. The studio patterned the Nancy Drew films after their successful B-movie series featuring another fictional female detective, resourceful reporter Torchy Blane, first played with sprightly wit by Glenda Farrell (succeeded by Lola Lane, then by a young Jane Wyman).

Miss Drew was still in high school, making her a cinematic rarity: an independent-minded teenage girl protagonist. Granville, an Oscar nominee for her work in *These Three* (1936), brings a plucky brattitude to the role. With a winning smile and an air of confidence, Nancy kicks off the movie by declaring her intention to be a lawyer someday, like her father, Carson Drew (John Litel). "I think every intelligent woman should have a career," she says, a slightly radical statement for a girl in the 1930s. When a wealthy dowager goes missing, Nancy builds a case out of mere suspicion while everyone advises her not to get involved. She disregards warnings and disobeys about a thousand rules, getting herself in hot water with the authorities. "Now, little girl, you'd better go back to the kindergarten and play with your dollies," the inept policeman Captain Tweedy tells her. Mortified, Nancy rises to the challenge,

Bonita Granville, 1938

Bonita Granville pushes Frankie Thomas and John Litel into danger.

"I guess it's just my woman's intuition. Every woman has one, you know."

—"NANCY DREW"

determined not only to solve the crime but also to prove she's more capable than he is.

In souping up the books, Warner Bros. made some modifications for the screen. Nancy's beau, Ned Nickerson, becomes Ted; her housekeeper, Hannah, becomes Effie; and Nancy is given a few quirky catchphrases. "What a character!" (said derisively about Captain Tweedy) and "I'll bet you $23.80 . . ." (the average weekly paycheck for a Works Progress Administration worker during the Depression) found their way into her vernacular. On film, Nancy has scatterbrained moments, during which she relies on Ted's cool logic. In the books, she is

less a comedienne and more an unleashed tigress with plenty of logic of her own.

Before the novels were revised in 1959 to make her character more polite, submissive, and older (eighteen), Nancy Drew was a whip-smart sixteen-year-old hellion with a passion for mystery and her own car, something few teens had at that time. The Nancy of the original books by Carolyn Keene (the pen name for a few different writers) was nothing short of remarkable. A bold adventuress who gallivants around River Heights in the dead of night, armed with nothing more than brains, a flashlight, and spike heels (which she uses to break a

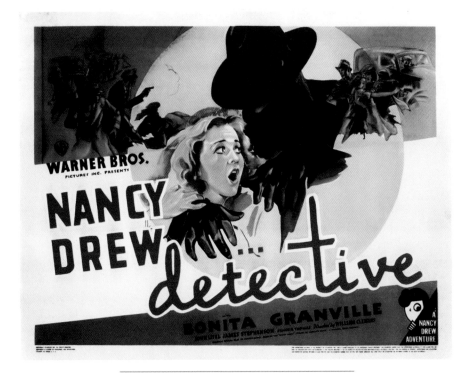

A lobby card featuring Bonita Granville as Nancy Drew

window and escape in one book), she was a powerful role model for millions of girls, daring them to dream bigger and braver.

Edward Stratemeyer of the Stratemeyer Syndicate (creator of the Hardy Boys series) dreamed up Nancy in 1929 and sent a memo to his staff describing his vision: "An up-to-date American girl at her best, bright, clever, resourceful, and full of energy." In the hands of the first "Carolyn Keene," author Mildred Wirt Benson—a former reporter and the first woman to earn a master's degree in journalism from the University of Iowa—Nancy became sassier and more self-reliant than Stratemeyer envisioned.

Nancy Drew ... Detective was followed by *Nancy Drew ... Reporter* (1939), *Nancy Drew ... Troubleshooter* (1939), and *Nancy Drew and the Hidden Staircase* (1939). The fun came to an end when Bonita Granville left Warners for MGM, and Nancy Drew was neglected until her revival in a 1970s TV series, a 2007 movie with Emma Roberts, and a new, more faithful adaptation of *Nancy Drew and the Hidden Staircase* by director Katt Shea in 2019, starring Sophia Lillis as Nancy.

Did You Know?

In 1947, Bonita Granville married producer Jack Wrather, and the two cofounded a production company. The first film they produced was the gritty grade-B noir *The Guilty,* in which Granville played a good twin and a bad twin. Also cast was John Litel, her father in the Nancy Drew films.

Joan Fontaine
AS "JANE EYRE"

Jane Eyre (1943)

"Oh. You have a will of your own," observes Orson Welles as Edward Rochester when he first encounters Jane Eyre. His tone of voice implies both respect and surprise. After all, a young woman with a will of her own was a novelty in early Victorian-era England. And Jane is nothing if not willful. As a girl, she rebels violently against her harsh upbringing, and as a woman, she demands equality and respect from her employer (and eventual husband) Mr. Rochester, though he's a wealthy gentleman and she a penniless orphan with nothing to her name but pride.

Author Charlotte Brontë knew a thing or two about willful women, being one herself. A century ahead of her time, she had a fiery, independent spirit that chafed at her society's anemic expectations of the fairer sex. Her literary heroine was an extension of herself: poor, petite, plain, and peeved. Through Jane, Brontë expressed her own opinions: "Women feel just as men feel; they need exercise for their faculties and a field for their efforts as much as their brothers do." When she published *Jane Eyre* in 1847, it was under the pen name Currer Bell. Jane was such a radical character— and a woman who wrote professionally was so frowned upon in her era—that Brontë hid behind a male moniker until the novel was a best seller.

As embodied by Joan Fontaine in Robert Stevenson's 1943 adaptation, Brontë's literary heroine takes on a touch of Hollywood glamour, with plenty of shadows falling across her face in a Gothic noir style. Though, arguably, none of the many screen versions of the book (widely considered to be the first feminist novel) succeed in fully illustrating Jane's formidable willpower, Stevenson's effort admirably attempts to stay faithful to its source. The early scenes feature Jane as a properly defiant child (played by Peggy Ann Garner) who is forced by the cruel school supervisor Mr. Brocklehurst to march in the pouring rain wearing a sign that reads "Rebellious." Also being punished is Jane's friend Helen, played by an eleven-year-old Elizabeth Taylor in one of her earliest roles. Years later, when Brocklehurst accuses Jane of ingratitude, she lashes out, "What have I to be grateful for?"

As governess at the spooky old mansion

Joan Fontaine as Jane Eyre in *Jane Eyre*

Orson Welles and Joan Fontaine

"Do you think because I'm poor and obscure and plain that I am soulless and heartless? I have as much soul as you and fully as much heart. And if God had gifted me with wealth and beauty, I should have made it as hard for you to leave me as it is now for me to leave you."

—"JANE EYRE"

of Thornfield, her forthright manner and strength of character earn Mr. Rochester's love, though he is pursued by many more glamorous and coquettish ladies than she. "You inquired of my feelings as an equal," she tells him; they share a connection that makes them mental and emotional equals. While investigating mysterious shrieks in the night, the cool-headed governess valiantly saves her employer's life when his bed is engulfed by fire.

It is when Jane falls in love with Edward that the film softens her character into a much more meek and submissive bride-to-be than is found in the novel. When he showers her with presents, the literary Jane feels "degradation" because she has no riches of her own. Fontaine's Jane,

Young Jane (Peggy Ann Garner) defends herself against her cousin, the bullying John Reed (Ronald Harris).

who always speaks in a whisper, appears delighted with her wedding gifts. She wisely walks out, though, when she learns of Edward's mad wife in the attic.

In the end, Jane finally agrees to marry Edward—after his wife dies and he is badly injured in a fire, his physical strength impaired. The movie's most egregious omission is the novel's crucial twist where Jane inherits a small fortune before she returns to Thornfield. Only when she and Edward are equals will she submit to a partnership.

After playing a naïve bride in *The Women* (1939), an insecure young wife in *Rebecca* (1940), a sickly fourteen-year-old in *The Constant Nymph* (1943), and the soft-spoken heroine in *Jane Eyre,* Joan Fontaine (born Joan de Havilland, younger sister of Olivia) was in danger of becoming typecast as Hollywood's resident good little girl. Then, in 1947, she added a new dimension to her image with *Ivy,* in which she played a scheming seductress. Fontaine continued the trend as nasty covert-manipulator Christabel Caine in Nicholas Ray's tour-de-force femme noir *Born to be Bad* (1950). In 1957's *Island in the Sun,* she became the first Caucasian actress to kiss an actor of color (Harry Belafonte) in a major film. The movie was banned by many theaters in the South, and Fontaine received death threats in the mail, which she reported to the FBI.

Did You Know?

Joan Fontaine was something of a daredevil in private life. "I've flown in an international balloon race. I've piloted my own plane. I've ridden to the hounds. I've done a lot of exciting things," she reflected in her later years.

Ingrid Bergman
AS "PAULA ALQUIST ANTON"

Gaslight (1944)

Early in *Gaslight*, the young, impressionable Paula tells her suitor, Gregory, that she wants to go away alone for a week to decide if she should marry him. She is wary of happiness. "I haven't had enough," she tells him, "and I feel I can't trust it." Following the stalker handbook to the letter, Gregory trails her out of town and is waiting for her when she arrives. This should have been Paula's first clue that she was dealing with a dangerous, manipulative control freak. But she desperately wants to believe the happiness she feels is real. She marries him anyway.

Thus begins the troubled union of Paula Alquist and Gregory Anton in George Cukor's atmospheric Edwardian-era thriller *Gaslight*, the 1944 film adaptation of a play by Patrick Hamilton. It's the movie that earned Ingrid Bergman her first Best Actress Academy Award, and it remains relevant in our culture seventy-five years later as the source of the psychological term *gaslighting*.

MGM's Louis B. Mayer originally planned to cast Hedy Lamarr as Paula, until a tall, talented, and beautiful Swedish import rocked the motion-picture colony as Ilsa Lund in *Casablanca* (1942) and Maria in *For Whom the Bell Tolls* (1943), among other indelible performances. To play a woman kept a virtual prisoner in a dark Gothic house, a victim of psychological abuse at the hands of her calculating husband (deliciously played against type by Charles Boyer), Bergman prepared by visiting mental hospitals and studying the body language of the afflicted. Paula is a difficult character for an actress to pull off; she must convey enough vulnerability to convince the audience that she's extremely susceptible to the power of suggestion, yet she must also possess an inner strength potent enough to eventually turn the tables on Gregory. Bergman had the right combination: an external fragility with a sturdy inner core, fortified by her difficult early life—her mother died when she was three, and she lost her father at age thirteen. Lonely and withdrawn, she flourished in the make-believe world of the theater.

Under the guidance of celebrated "woman's director" Cukor, Bergman's acting in *Gaslight* is sublime. As Paula grows increas-

Ingrid Bergman as Paula Alquist Anton in *Gaslight*

> "Because I am mad, I hate you. Because I am mad, I have betrayed you. And because I am mad, I am rejoicing in my heart without a shred of pity, without a shred of regret—watching you go with glory in my heart!"
>
> —"PAULA ALQUIST ANTON"

ingly confounded by several mysteries—her sudden forgetfulness, the strange noises coming from the attic, and the dimming of the gaslights—Bergman quietly builds to a frighteningly real emotional breakdown using the subtlest nuances and facial expressions. *"Gaslight* was one of my favorite films," she later said, "and one of the greatest experiences of my life." Her female costars were top-notch: Dame May Whitty as a nosy neighbor and seventeen-year-old Angela Lansbury in her Oscar-nominated screen debut as the Antons' surly parlor maid.

Gaslight is one in a wave of paranoid mystery films that included Alfred Hitchcock's *Rebecca* (1940) and *Suspicion* (1941), both starring Joan Fontaine; *Undercurrent* (1946) with Katharine Hepburn and Robert Taylor; and *The Secret Beyond the Door* (1948) with Joan Bennett and Michael Redgrave. In these movies, the protagonist is a young, newly married woman who questions her husband's trustworthiness. Paula in *Gaslight* begins to doubt her own sanity as Gregory verbally bullies her into submission. By the time she fights to break free from his mind control, he has already broken her will. Thankfully, handsome Joseph Cotten is lurking in the shadows, waiting to add the final piece to the puzzle.

Today, gaslighting is recognized as a form of abuse in which the victim is cunningly manipulated into questioning his or her own grasp of reality. Because women are traditionally believed to be trusting and compliant, they are the targets of gaslighting more often than men. In Paula's case, she becomes empowered once she learns the painful truth that there was "nothing real from the beginning" about her husband's love. Standing over the bound Gregory and taunting him with a knife, she pays back some of the torment he put her through by engaging in a little gaslighting herself.

Ingrid Bergman and Angela Lansbury consult the script.

Offscreen, Ingrid Bergman was a staunch individualist who lived life on her own terms. In 1950, she was ostracized by Hollywood and the rest of the world for doing publicly what many of them did in private: trapped in an unhappy marriage, she fell in love with the married director Roberto Rossellini on the set of the film *Stromboli* (1950), and they had a child out of wedlock. She held her head high through the scandal, marrying and eventually divorcing Rossellini and returning to Hollywood to win two more Oscars.

Did You Know?

George Cukor discovered Angela Lansbury behind the counter at Bullock's Wilshire department store in Los Angeles, where she had a part-time job wrapping Christmas gifts. She had no dramatic training when he cast her in the film.

Charles Boyer and Ingrid Bergman in their tense final confrontation

Grace Kelly

AS "LISA FREMONT"

Rear Window (1954)

As fashionista Lisa Fremont, Grace Kelly sets *Rear Window* on fire with her beauty, wit, and smoldering sex appeal. Cool blonde perfection on the outside and hot-blooded on the inside, Lisa fits the description director Alfred Hitchcock once applied to Grace: "a snow-covered volcano." In her introductory scene—one of the most famous in movie history—she swoops down on James Stewart's L.B. "Jeff" Jefferies like a seductive bird of prey while he sleeps in his wheelchair, his broken leg rendering him vulnerable. When her fire-engine red lips meet his, he barely knows what hit him.

But Lisa Fremont is oh-so-much more than just the hero's hot girlfriend. She's one of the new self-sufficient breed of working women who emerged during World War II. A power player in the fashion industry, Lisa has her own money, her own career, and is used to getting her own way. In a role reversal rare for the 1950s, Lisa sweeps in from work, dressed to the nines and chattering about her job, while Jeff sits at home in his pajamas. She also decides to spend the night at her boyfriend's place without consulting him or anyone else. "Surprise," she purrs, "is the most important element of attack."

The short story that served as the basis for *Rear Window,* "It Had to Be Murder" by Cornell Woolrich, has no major female characters, only a single disabled man who spies on his neighbors from his apartment window. Hitchcock and screenwriter John Michael Hayes added two strong women to the mix: Lisa and Stella, Jeff's nurse, played for comic relief by the sassy Thelma Ritter. Grace Kelly's own personality (and a dash of Hayes's wife) informed the character of Lisa. As Hayes got to know Grace, he sensed a bold determination and powerful will beneath the refined exterior. Miss Kelly had fled her cushy life in Philadelphia high society at eighteen to strike out on her own as an actress, though her wealthy parents refused to support her, telling her she'd never make it. But no force on earth could stop Grace Kelly from following her heart.

Inspired by Grace's dual fire-and-ice nature, Lisa Fremont became an enticing hybrid of two female film-noir archetypes:

Grace Kelly as Lisa Fremont in *Rear Window*

James Stewart and Grace Kelly team up to solve a mystery.

> ## "You're not up on your private eye literature. When they're in trouble, it's always their girl Friday who gets them out of it."
> —"LISA FREMONT"

the deadly femme fatale and the innocuous girlfriend/wife. Lisa is not a bad girl, but she's no passive innocent, either.

In taking it upon herself to scale a fire escape and explore the murderer's lair (in high heels and a full-skirted dress, naturally), Lisa turns the tables on the expected movie clichés. Because Jeff is confined to a wheelchair, by necessity Lisa becomes his "legs," and—as Hitchcock and Peter Bogdanovich agreed in their 1963 interview—the "dominant partner in the relationship." As the rear-window mystery consumes Lisa, she gets so excited by the thrill of chasing down

a murderer that she can't keep her mind on anything else. Despite her fashion-model appearance, she was born to play sleuth.

But her daring actions provoke disapproval from two men: the cantankerous Jeff, who constantly criticizes her for being "too perfect," and police detective Lieutenant Doyle. Typically, when a male detective relies on hunches, it means he has a sharp and perceptive mind. When a woman has the same kind of hunch, it must be labeled "feminine intuition," which is the pejorative term Doyle uses to dismiss Lisa's contributions.

At the end of *Rear Window*, Lisa's feminine intuition is proved correct. If she hadn't done a little breaking and entering, there would have been no evidence of murder. In fact, without her and Stella's intervention, the investigation would have ended with Doyle's declaration that "there is no case." By acting the hero on behalf of the wounded Jeff, Lisa steps into his shoes and uses her own mind to solve the mystery. Case closed.

Did You Know?

James Stewart's memories of *Rear Window* were focused on his glamorous costar. "We were all so crazy about Grace Kelly," Stewart recalled. "Everyone just sat around and waited for her to come in the morning, so we could just look at her. Me included."

Grace Kelly, Alfred Hitchcock, and script supervisor Peggy Robertson on the set of *Rear Window*

Jodie Foster

AS "CLARICE STARLING"

The Silence of the Lambs (1991)

Before *The Silence of the Lambs* became part of our cultural landscape in 1991, it seemed improbable that a movie about a gruesome psychopath who preys on women would present such a powerful female protagonist. As FBI trainee Clarice Starling, Jodie Foster elevates the horror-movie heroine to new heights as she bravely hunts down the dangerous serial killer Buffalo Bill (Ted Levine) with the aid of another dangerous serial killer, Hannibal Lecter (Anthony Hopkins).

Women cops, even FBI agents, had certainly been seen in previous movies. But a young woman who is the driving force behind catching the bad guy, especially one with the insight, courage, and depth of Clarice, was—and still is—as uncommon as a four-leaf clover. Director Jonathan Demme was extremely conscious of telling the dark tale from a woman's perspective, even describing his vision for the film as "a feminist piece." To this end, he has Tak Fujimoto's camera follow Clarice through a world that is largely the domain of men: her male boss, male colleagues, and the male criminals with whom she interacts are shot in close-ups tight enough to make the audience fidget. In the 1970s, film critic Laura Mulvey coined the term "the male gaze" to describe the common cinematic objectification of women from a heterosex-ual male perspective. Rarely, if ever, has the male gaze been subverted as effectively on film as in *The Silence of the Lambs*. Viewers are made to understand how Clarice feels as she fends off relentless leering and flirtations in order to do her job. "Are you hitting on me, doctor?" she rhetorically asks an entomologist who assists her with the case. When FBI director Crawford (Scott Glenn) engages in sexist behavior as a ruse to gain the confidence of a small-town sheriff, Starling calls him on it. "Cops look at you to see how to act," she reminds him. "It matters."

According to screenwriter Ted Tally, the author of the original novel, Thomas Harris, challenged himself to "try to live inside the mind of a female character, to put a woman at the center of a book," and Tally stayed true to this objective. Clarice's

Jodie Foster as Clarice Starling in *The Silence of the Lambs* most admirable quality may be that she's not a one-dimensional woman of steel, but a human being who is visibly shaken by the violent crimes she encounters, and who perseveres regardless. As John Wayne once said, "Courage is being scared to death, but saddling up anyway."

Jodie Foster and director Jonathan Demme share a joke on set.

"You see a lot, doctor. But are you strong enough to point that high-powered perception at yourself? What about it? Why don't you look at yourself and write down what you see? Maybe you're afraid to."

—"CLARICE STARLING"

When Demme came on board, he had Michelle Pfeiffer in mind as Clarice, but Jodie Foster had other ideas. The former child actress, Yale graduate, and Oscar winner for *The Accused* (1988) was determined to land the role. "I know I'm not your first choice," she told Demme frankly, "but I'm going to play this part." For Foster, who had portrayed her share of victims (Iris in *Taxi Driver* [1976], for one), "There was a sort of healing process, and almost a growing-up process to finally playing the woman who saves women," she later

said. The woman Clarice saves is not the standard helpless victim, either; abductee Catherine Martin (Brooke Smith) puts up an admirable fight for her life. Catherine's mother (Diane Baker) and Clarice's confidante Ardelia (Kasi Lemmons) round out the supporting cast of tough ladies.

As the brilliantly twisted Dr. Lecter, Hopkins has the greatest lines and received the most media attention, though he only appears in the film for a total of twenty-six minutes. Clarice is the movie's solid moral core, the quiet, working-class vessel of law enforcement—not the kind of part that typically garners awards. But win awards she did: an Academy Award, a Golden Globe, a BAFTA, and many more. Since then, Jodie Foster has played several other remarkable women, including a gifted scientist in *Contact* (1997), an intrepid single mom in

Panic Room (2002), and a livid vigilante in *The Brave One* (2007). Always challenging herself to take risks, Foster founded her own production company and branched out into directing with *Little Man Tate* in 1991, later helming *Money Monster* (2017) with George Clooney and Julia Roberts.

Over a quarter-century after *The Silence of the Lambs*, Clarice Starling remains an exceptional character in the actress's oeuvre. Like a mythical hero, she descends into a dark labyrinth to rescue a kidnapped prin-cess from a monster—traditionally a man's role. As Foster herself has observed of Clarice, "I think this is a great American hero."

Did You Know?

Off camera, Jodie Foster and Anthony Hopkins didn't speak at all during production of the film. "He was petrifying," Foster recalled in 2017. "He was absolutely so scary that I couldn't bring myself to talk to him."

Anthony Hopkins, Jodie Foster, and Scott Glenn

Strong Survivors

Come hell or high water, these are women who stick it out to
the bitter end. They may have seemingly insurmountable odds
stacked against them, but they stand up to the challenge and fight,
often alone or with little help from others. By nature, they are good.
But—forced by circumstances beyond their control—they may resort
to whatever is necessary to stay alive. Long live their perseverance.

Vivien Leigh
AS "SCARLETT O'HARA"

Gone with the Wind (1939)

"Oh, if I just wasn't a lady what I wouldn't tell that varmint!"

Come on, Scarlett. Who do you think you're fooling? We all know that your "fiddle-dee-dee" Southern gentility is just an act. Beneath your flouncy bonnets and frilly hoop-skirts dwells a bold egotist, a savvy entrepreneur, and a deft manipulator, supported by a core of ironclad determination. Above all else, you are a survivor.

When Atlanta native Margaret Mitchell started writing the sweeping historical novel she initially called *Tomorrow Is Another Day,* she planned to make honorable homemaker Melanie Hamilton Wilkes her heroine. But something unexpected happened: the fiery, obstinate, selfish character of Katie Scarlett O'Hara took over, pushing her way to the forefront as if hell-bent on claiming her rightful place at center stage. After Hollywood producer David O. Selznick's assistant, Kay Brown, convinced him to buy the screen rights in 1936, Selznick spent $50,000 and two and a half years searching for Scarlett, only to finally find her in little-known British actress Vivien Leigh.

Leigh did not fall into the role of a lifetime by chance; she was obsessed with playing Scarlett. She read and reread passages in the novel describing its heroine and practiced in front of her mirror for hours, intent on flying to Los Angeles and knocking Selznick's socks off, which she did. She looked the part, but more than that, Leigh "invested Scarlett with something beyond beauty," according to film critic Molly Haskell, "something altogether uncanny—a demonic energy, a feverishness that would later tip over into illness and pathology." Costar Olivia de Havilland remembered Leigh giving more of herself to the movie "than it ever gave back to her."

Ladylike on the outside, Scarlett seethes with a spirit of rebellion. Perhaps because Mitchell wrote the novel between 1926 and 1936, her heroine seems a daring, self-sufficient 1920s–1930s woman trapped in the conventions of the antebellum South. She starts a lumber business (and refuses to give it up when Rhett asks her to), becomes independently wealthy, and drives her own horse and buggy through town unescorted (scandalous!).

It's in a crisis that we see what Scarlett

Vivien Leigh as Scarlett O'Hara in *Gone with the Wind*

Vivien Leigh and Hattie McDaniel

"As God is my witness, they're not going to lick me.
I'm going to live through this, and when it's all over, I'll never be
hungry again. No, nor any of my folks. If I have to lie, steal, cheat,
or kill. As God is my witness, I'll never be hungry again!"

—"SCARLETT O'HARA"

is really made of. Engulfed by the hell of war, she delivers Melly's child without a doctor (though she mutters under her breath, "Melanie, I hate you, and I hate your baby!"), drives them through the burning ruins of Atlanta alone, shoots a Yankee pillager point-blank in the face without flinching, and, when he dies, rolls him for every cent he's got like an expert pickpocket. Ashley (Leslie Howard), a soldier who survived the atrocities of the Civil War, admits he's a coward compared to Scarlett, telling her with a touch of envy, "You don't know the meaning of fear."

Mammy is the only woman in the film with enough gumption to stand up to spitfire Scarlett, serving as the much-needed voice of unvarnished truth and common sense. "It's no use trying to sweet-talk me, Miss Scarlett," she roars. "I knows you ever since I put the first pair of diapers on you!" Although the film's cringe-inducing depiction of willing, obedient slaves has aged badly, Hattie McDaniel's performance as Mammy is timeless. McDaniel, whose parents were former slaves and who had worked as a domestic before carving out a lucrative Hollywood career, made history as the first African American recipient of an Oscar for her portrayal.

Gone with the Wind is full of heroic women, from shrewd Belle Watling to Scarlett's "goodie-goodie" frenemy Melanie, who charges downstairs with a sword when Tara is invaded, though she's so weak from childbirth she can barely walk. Olivia de Havilland has proven to be an awe-inspiring survivor in real life, too, outliving all of her costars and shifting the Hollywood power structure with her landmark 1944 lawsuit. The de Havilland Law limits the ability of powerful studios to unfairly bind performers to long-term contracts, and it eventually helped to topple the entire studio system.

For all its legendary grandeur and its ten Oscars, it's important to note that *Gone with the Wind* is what Hollywood insiders used to refer to as a "woman's picture," the kind they stopped making by the early 1960s. And it's the greatest, most epic woman's picture of them all. Its protagonist—love her or hate her—has inspired millions of women and men to keep going in hard times. No matter what life throws her way, Scarlett is never defeated.

Did You Know?

Though Vivien Leigh was pleased with *Gone with the Wind*, she privately complained to friends that its running time of nearly four hours was "hard on one's ass."

Vivien Leigh signs her *Gone with the Wind* contract as David O. Selznick, Leslie Howard, and Olivia de Havilland look on.

Sigourney Weaver

AS "ELLEN RIPLEY"

Alien (1979) and *Aliens* (1986)

In the days before *Alien*, science-fiction movies were commonly told from a man's point of view. Think of those 1950s pictures where a rocket ship of astronauts lands on a distant planet to find a population of curvaceous, love-starved women who have never set eyes on Earth men (see *Queen of Outer Space* and *Missile to the Moon*, both from 1958). With a few exceptions, outer space was usually the realm of male fantasy.

Then along came Ellen Ripley, warrant officer aboard the starship *Nostromo*, an intelligent, authoritative character who was originally written—like all the characters in the film—to be played by either a man or a woman. A 1979 *Photoplay* article observed that Sigourney Weaver "reveled in the triumphant little swell of feminism" *Alien* caused not only by presenting equality between the male and female crew members, but also by placing a woman in the heroic leading role typically embodied by a man. This is exactly what drew struggling stage actress Weaver to the script, and she won the part over several well-known male actors, including John Travolta. When director Ridley Scott and producer Alan Ladd Jr. decided to cast a woman as Ripley, not one word of dialogue was changed. "There's nothing feminine in the lines," Weaver noted.

The other woman in the crew is Lambert, played by Veronica Cartwright.

Though a capable crewmember, Lambert has emotional outbursts of squealing and crying—and who could blame her, given the slimy xenomorphs they encounter? But Ripley, by comparison, is cool as ice. Her voice never wavers, her eye contact never drops when she confronts the android Ash about disobeying her direct orders and letting the deadly extraterrestrial on board. "When Dallas and Kane are off the ship, I'm senior officer," she reminds him. ("Oh yes, I forgot," Ash mumbles unconvincingly.) Captain Dallas takes Ash's side, and Ripley is appalled. "I don't trust him," she says, and warns everybody of the danger she senses, but they don't take her concerns as seriously as they could—which is why she is the only team member who survives in the end.

In her feature film debut, Weaver's performance is intensely credible when, after a crushing realization that the *Nostromo*

Sigourney Weaver as Ellen Ripley in *Alien*

workers are considered expendable by the company they work for, she seizes Ash by the shirt collar, slams him against a wall, and throttles the smug expression off his face. Ripley is logical, efficient, and tough, but beneath her green uniform beats a human heart; she risks her life to save the cat, Jonesy, who becomes her final friend and ally. Virtually overnight, *Alien* shuttled Weaver from unknown to A-list star.

━━━◇━━━

"You're going out there to destroy them, right? Not to study, not to bring back, but to wipe them out?"

—"ELLEN RIPLEY"

━━━◇━━━

In 1986, James Cameron sent Ellen Ripley back to asteroid LV-426 in his pumped-up sequel *Aliens*. Cameron gave her a deceased daughter and a surrogate child in Newt (Carrie Henn), an orphaned girl traumatized by monsters, the only survivor of a small colony. This may have been unnecessary (does Ripley really need a thwarted maternal instinct to be a heroic woman?), but it's effective. Instead of a cat, Ripley is driven to save the life of a little girl, leading to a classic showdown with one big, bad alien mama—the queen of the hive. When Ripley straps herself into a power loader, stares down the queen, and

threatens, "Get away from her, you bitch," the first major female action hero had officially arrived. Weaver also became the first Best Actress nominee the Oscars recognized for a science-fiction film.

For *Aliens*, Cameron brought along his *Terminator* leading man Michael Biehn (as good guy Hicks) and the producer of *The Terminator* (1984), Gale Anne Hurd, who has since become one of the most successful and respected film and TV producers in the industry. Weaver returned to space for *Alien 3* in 1992, and teamed with Winona Ryder for *Alien Resurrection* in 1997. In 1999, she had some fun at the expense of her sci-fi superhero image as TV actress Gwen DiMarco in the spaced-out comedy *Galaxy Quest*.

Ripley's hard-as-nails legacy has inspired and encouraged a generation of actresses to play tougher, less sentimental roles. Jennifer Lawrence in the *Hunger Games* franchise, Kate Beckinsale in the *Underworld* series, and Charlize Theron in *Mad Max: Fury Road* (2015) and *Atomic Blonde* (2017) have all acknowledged Sigourney Weaver for forging the path they followed.

Did You Know?

Sigourney Weaver had a hard time coming to terms with the automatic weapons she uses in *Aliens*. "I found those scenes quite difficult," she said in 1986. "I would stand there thinking, 'Here I am a member of the gun control lobby in a picture where I do nothing but shoot guns.'"

DYNAMIC DAMES

Top: Director Ridley Scott and Weaver on the set of *Alien*. Bottom: Sigourney Weaver heads up the cast of *Aliens*.

Whoopi Goldberg

AS "CELIE"

The Color Purple (1985)

After proving they could crank out blockbusters like nobody's business, director Steven Spielberg and producer Kathleen Kennedy branched out from extraterrestrials and Indiana Jones to bring Alice Walker's Pulitzer Prize–winning novel *The Color Purple* to the screen in 1985. Whoopi Goldberg made her dramatic screen debut as Walker's quiet, downtrodden heroine Celie. From there, Goldberg found major fame as a standup comic, TV personality, and movie star, succeeding Hattie McDaniel as the second woman of color to win an Oscar (for her role in *Ghost* [1990]).

As if that weren't enough, the film gave Oprah Winfrey her first acting role as the proud, outspoken Sofia. Also featuring Desreta Jackson, Akosua Busia, Margaret Avery, and Rae Dawn Chong, *The Color Purple* was a highly unusual mainstream movie for its day, one that celebrates the lives of African American women.

As a girl in early-1900s Georgia, Celie is legally free but is treated no better than a slave. After bearing two children by her stepfather by the tender age of fourteen, Celie is "given" to Mister (Danny Glover), a widower with a brood of unruly kids. Celie longs to be with the "only somebody in the world" who loves her—her sister, Nettie. When Mister forces the girls apart, Celie spends miserable

decades dominated by his cruel physical and mental abuse. "You're black, you're poor, you're ugly, you're a woman," he tells her. "You ain't nothin' at all."

During these difficult years, Celie undergoes an incredible evolution. Slowly, painfully, bit by precious bit, she absorbs education and self-worth, despite Mister's attempts to break her spirit. As she matures, she learns from two substitute sisters: Sofia and the dynamic Shug Avery. A juke-joint chanteuse, Shug is as shiny as a firecracker and as free as the wind; she's everything that Celie is not. As Celie basks in attention from Shug, she blooms like one of the purple flowers in the field.

Critic Roger Ebert credited the film's

Whoopi Goldberg as Celie in *The Color Purple*

Whoopi Goldberg and Steven Spielberg on location in North Carolina

"I'm poor, black . . . I may even be ugly. But, dear God, I'm here. I'm here."

—"CELIE"

greatness to Goldberg's performance as Celie. "The scene where she is coaxed and persuaded and finally teased into smiling is the turning point of the story," he wrote, "and one of those moments when we see humanity shining out of the screen upon us." Once Shug gives her a lesson in love, Celie finds the courage to go on, and eventually to tell Mister off and leave him forever—but not before a harrowing sequence in which her silent fury boils over and she almost slits his throat with a razor. Instead, she allows him to live, but curses him: "Until you do right by me, everything you even think about gonna fail." Liberated from her oppressor, Celie not only survives, but thrives and finds joy in her life. She owns her own land, runs a successful shop (making the ultimate statement for equality with her "folkspants,"

slacks made for men and women of all sizes), and is reunited with her family.

Spielberg's film was a critical and commercial winner, but it faced controversy when the NAACP joined the Coalition Against Blaxploitation to protest its unflattering depiction of African American men. The women do indeed get preferential treatment; the men are portrayed as bumbling jackasses at best and sadistic rapists at worst. But the film's purpose is not to condemn black men; it's to tell Celie's story. As Oprah Winfrey once observed, "The movie was not for or against men. It's egotistical and macho for men to even think it's about them. *The Color Purple* is a novel about women."

Years after the film's release, Alice Walker revealed to the *Los Angeles Times* the strain she suffered under "the severe criticism, bashing, [and] trashing" of her book and her decision to sell the rights to Spielberg. The author, poet, and activist leveled a few of her own criticisms at the film, but wrote in 1996, "Though *The Color Purple* is not what many wished, it is more than many hoped, or had seen on a movie screen before. It still moves me after all these years, as I relive the feeling of love that was palpable daily on the set."

Walker's novel was adapted into a stage musical in 2005. After its acclaimed three-year run on Broadway, it was revived in 2015 and has since been performed around the world.

Did You Know?

Spielberg staged an unconventional audition for Whoopi Goldberg, inviting her to perform a standup show before "a few of his friends" in Los Angeles. "A few of his friends!" Goldberg recalled. "Do you know who his friends are? There were eighty people in the room. Michael Jackson was there."

Celie takes a stand against Mister (Danny Glover) at the dinner table.

Geena Davis
AS "THELMA"
Susan Sarandon
AS "LOUISE"

Thelma & Louise (1991)

Thelma & Louise **may be the definitive women's empowerment** film and the most in-your-face feminist fable we've seen yet from a major Hollywood studio (MGM). Its very existence is a minor miracle. When music-video producer Callie Khouri wrote her first screenplay in 1988, she had no idea if it would get made; she just felt compelled to tell a story. "I wanted to show that feeling of what it's like to be in this world that wants you to be less than you are," Khouri recalled in 2014. "I wanted to write a movie about what the world looked like from the front seat of that car." In doing so, she would become one in a handful of women to win the Academy Award for Best Screenplay.

Her script made it to Mimi Polk, who ran director/producer Ridley Scott's company. Though Scott was intrigued by the story's possibilities, several other male filmmakers turned the project down flat; one described Thelma and Louise as "basically detestable and unsympathetic," and another dismissed them as "two bitches in a car." Scott decided the only way to get the movie made was to direct it himself. He worked with Khouri on pumping up the script's humor to appeal to a wider audience, telling her, "Comedies are so powerful....You want the males to listen. You want them to actually eat crow." The result was a bittersweet blend of laughter and tears.

Khouri had Holly Hunter and Frances McDormand in mind for the leads (Scott envisioned Jodie Foster and Michelle Pfeiffer), but the perfect chemistry was struck with Geena Davis as scattered housewife Thelma and Susan Sarandon as cynical waitress Louise. Both actresses garnered Best Actress Oscar nominations for their bravura performances as two Arkansas girlfriends on the run from the law after their weekend trip gets shot—as does a barfly who tries to rape Thelma in a parking lot until Louise pulls the trigger.

Geena Davis as Thelma and Susan Sarandon as Louise in *Thelma & Louise*

> ## "Now, I swear, three days ago neither one of us would've ever pulled a stunt like this, but if you was ever to meet my husband, you'd understand why."
>
> —"THELMA"

The movie's magic lies in the subtle tonal shift that occurs somewhere along the dusty roads the ladies travel in their vintage Thunderbird convertible. As the scenery changes from the green South to the vast, golden Southwest, Thelma and Louise undergo a metamorphosis, becoming liberated from all that constricted them in the past. For the first time in her life, Thelma tells off the domineering clod she married at eighteen (and has a fling with an adorable drifter played by Brad Pitt in his first major role). Louise lets her hair down, discarding the cosmetics and transforming into a sun-scorched, wild-haired waif. By the end, both women scarcely resemble the selves they presented in the beginning. "I don't ever remember feeling this awake," Thelma says. Louise agrees.

It is an awakening born of crisis. As Janis Joplin sang, "Freedom's just another word for nothin' left to lose." As the law closes in, Thelma and Louise lose everything they once clung to—security, money, men, propriety, hope—allowing them to experience the exhilaration of true freedom. Once the women reach a point of no return, they go full-throttle vigilante, teaching a lesson at gunpoint to a truck driver who assaults them with crude sexual innuendo. "We think you have really bad manners," Thelma observes. "You say

you're sorry," Louise demands. When he refuses, they shoot his tires, then blast his oil rig. As it explodes in a blaze of glory, the women purge years of swallowed anger over being ogled, belittled, bossed, and generally taken advantage of by men.

Compassionate Agent Slocumb (Harvey Keitel) tries to intervene, but he can only do so much; the system is not stacked in the ladies' favor. The iconic final freeze-frame at the Grand Canyon is in keeping with their newfound power and liberation, because our female outlaws never surrender, ensuring the "happy ending" Scott wanted for his "heroes," as he called them.

Though it was an overwhelming success (earning over $45 million at the box office and six Oscar nods), the epic that should have incited a revolution barely made a dent in the Hollywood machine. After *Thelma & Louise*, Geena Davis told

Louise and Thelma embark on their road trip.

> ## "Where do you get off behaving like that with women you don't even know? Huh? How'd you feel if someone did that to your mother? Or your sister? Or your wife?"
> —"LOUISE"

♦

The Guardian in 2011, everyone said to her, "'This changes everything! There's going to be so many female buddy movies!' and nothing changed. And then the next movie I did was *A League of Their Own,* which was a huge hit and all the talk was, 'Well now, beyond a doubt, women's sports movies, we're going to see a wave of them.'…There was no trend whatsoever."

In response to this type of problem, in 2006 Davis founded the Geena Davis Institute on Gender in Media, a research-based organization that promotes gender balance in the entertainment industry. In 2014, Susan Sarandon revealed that she's received loads of fan mail over the years from women inspired by *Thelma & Louise.* "I think this idea of not settling speaks to a lot of people.…You have the option to rewrite the story that you're telling with your life, and that's what these women do."

Did You Know?

Sarandon and Davis had tremendous creative input on the film, from adding their own dialogue to certain scenes (like their admonishments to the trucker) to sneaking into the wardrobe department and dirtying up their T-shirts so they looked more road-trip authentic.

Top: Susan Sarandon. Bottom: Geena Davis and Jason Beghe

Angela Bassett

AS "TINA TURNER"

What's Love Got to Do With It (1993)

The extreme highs and lows of rock legend Tina Turner's incredible life journey were practically made for a movie screen. In 1993, Disney-owned Touchstone Pictures released *What's Love Got to Do With It*, a surprisingly raw biopic starring Angela Bassett in a spot-on, Oscar-nominated turn as "the hardest-working woman in rock and roll."

Based on Turner's 1986 autobiography *I, Tina,* the movie starts way back in 1940s Nutbush, Tennessee, where the themes in little Anna Mae Bullock's life are established: she's ousted from the church choir for singing with too much gusto, and her mother leaves her abusive father. At sixteen, she sees devilishly charismatic Ike Turner (Laurence Fishburne in a boldly unsympathetic role) rockin' onstage in St. Louis. When Anna grabs Ike's microphone and starts belting, it's obvious she's got star quality. "You are a woman, any man can see that," Ike tells her, "but it's like, you sang like a man." Before you can say "Proud Mary," she's joined his band, Ike changes her name to Tina without even consulting her, and the two have a baby (followed by a stack of hit records). He also begins physically abusing her, a pattern that continues throughout their fourteen-year marriage.

Soon the Turners are in a lopsided domestic arrangement. Tina sings her lungs out and dances up a sweat onstage every night—working just as hard as Ike—and during the day, she does the cooking, cleaning, and child rearing, not to mention putting up with Ike. Often high on drugs, he beats her and tells her that it's her fault. "I gave him manicures, pedicures, massages whenever he wanted them. And now I was even writing songs," Tina wrote of the waning days of their marriage. "But it was never enough."

"I remember how strenuous and arduous it was," Angela Bassett later recalled of her role, "physically, but also emotionally." Performing to Turner's actual voice (and wearing some of Turner's authentic fabulously fringed costumes), she packs a memorable punch. Twenty-five years after channeling Tina, Bassett made a mighty and majestic Queen Ramonda, T'Challa's

Angela Bassett as Tina Turner in *What's Love Got to Do With It*

mother and ruler of Wakanda, in *Black Panther* (2018). From there, she became the head of the CIA in *Mission Impossible— Fallout*. "I was raised by strong women. . . . I'm attempting to raise a strong daughter," she said in 2018, explaining the importance of powerful female characters.

•••••——◇——•••••

> ## "I just believe that anything is possible, you know. Anything. Now, it took me a long time to get Ike out of my system. And now that I've done that, I'm ready. I'm ready and I know what I want."
>
> —"TINA TURNER"

•••••——◇——•••••

Then twenty-eight, Kate Lanier wrote the screenplay without sanitizing the sordid aspects of Turner's life and went on to a steady screenwriting career that includes the Queen Latifah–starring comedy *Beauty Shop* (2005) and *CrazySexyCool: The TLC Story* (2013). Lanier's sharp dialogue cuts to the heart of the Turners' dysfunction: "Just like everybody else that I tried to help out my whole life, she done left me," Ike complains of his fifth wife. "I wouldn't do that," a still-teenage Tina responds.

Like many women in abusive relationships, Tina felt obligated to stay. But her promise to never leave became "harder and harder to keep," she said in 1993. "You

either try to kill yourself or you say, 'It's time to go.' I did both. I tried to kill myself. And I got out of there." One day in 1976, with thirty-six cents in her pocket, she leaves for good, relinquishing any rights to the joint fortune they amassed, or even royalties to the songs they recorded—in exchange for keeping the name Ike gave her. In 1984, on tour promoting her epic comeback album *Private Dancer*, Ike tries once more to intimidate her, appearing backstage with a gun, a nerve-wracking

Angela Bassett

scene in the movie. But a newly empowered Tina sees right through his tricks. "Is that supposed to scare me?" she scoffs. After all she's been through, this woman is fearless.

Rising phoenix-like from the ashes of the Ike and Tina Turner Revue, at forty-three she becomes a Grammy-winning living legend in her own right. The film ends on a happily-ever-after note, as this enlightened Buddhist survivor sells over twelve million records and performs sold-out concerts all over the world. She later entered into a happy union with German music executive Erwin Bach, and in 2018 her life story became *Tina: The Musical.*

Ike Turner ended up serving time in prison and dying of a cocaine overdose in 2007.

Did You Know?

Angela Bassett was chosen for the role over another contender named Halle Berry. Bassett's screen test consisted of performing "Proud Mary" in the style of Tina herself.

Angela Bassett and Laurence Fishburne

Jennifer Lawrence

AS "KATNISS EVERDEEN"

The Hunger Games films (2012–2015)

In the young-adult literature trade, it's long been an accepted fact that girls will read a book with a male protagonist, but boys generally won't read a book with a female protagonist. Former Nickelodeon TV-show writer Suzanne Collins shifted that paradigm with her best-selling *The Hunger Games,* a trilogy that has proven insanely popular with both girls and boys. Twenty-second-century tomboy Katniss Everdeen, a teenage girl with valor, skill, and a mighty moral core, drives the dystopian combat tales. "It's an unexpected choice," Collins has noted, to have "a female protagonist in a gladiator story."

When the novels were adapted for the big screen, the role of the Girl on Fire was given to a young actress on fire, Jennifer Lawrence. At twenty-two, Lawrence had already caused a sensation as a rugged survivalist in *Winter's Bone* (2010) and as a young Mystique in *X-Men: First Class* (2011) and was working on *Silver Linings Playbook* (2012), the film that would make her the second youngest Best Actress Oscar recipient in history. "I'm always finding myself drawn to strong characters," she has said, "probably because I want to be like that." Lawrence's talent and fame, combined with Collins's vision, have made Katniss the box office's most lucrative female action hero of all time.

Projecting the reality-TV trend to its perverse conclusion, *The Hunger Games* follows randomly "reaped" contestants in a televised fight to the death. When her younger sister, Prim, is chosen, Katniss volunteers to go in her place and wins. Neither media savvy nor a people pleaser, Katniss survives because she's an accomplished hunter/forager by necessity—she's been her family's breadwinner since her father died in a mining accident when she was eleven—and because, to an audience used to being spoon-fed manufactured reality, she's refreshingly real. So real that her obvious disdain for the autocratic government makes her a threat to the Capitol. "She has become a beacon of hope for the

Jennifer Lawrence as Katniss Everdeen

Katniss draws her bow.

> "I'm going to kill Snow. Nothing good is safe while he's alive. And I can't make another speech about it. No more cameras. No more propos. No more Games. He needs to see my eyes when I kill him."
>
> —"KATNISS EVERDEEN"

Rebellion," President Snow (Donald Sutherland) says in *Catching Fire* (2013), "and she must be eliminated." By the end of *Mockingjay Part 2* (2015), Katniss has become the one who must eliminate *him*.

Only there to save her sister's life, Katniss is already a step ahead of the other Tributes; she exhibits the qualities of courage (willingly sacrificing her life for another) and determinism (taking her fate into her own hands). Lawrence was drawn to these traits when she fell in love with the books. "I love that she's a warrior for people," the actress has said. "She's a Joan of Arc, a fighter. She's

one of the first people to stand up to the Capitol." In standing up for herself, Katniss incites a revolution, making her a powerful role model for young women.

This chick can rock flaming gowns like an *haute couture* model if need be, but outer appearances mean little to her. A complex female character, she is not overly beautified or sexualized, but rather is judged by her deeds and her inner strength. Her weakness? "I've never been very good at friends," she admits.

Although this survivor starts as a lone wolf—her only close friend being Gale

(Liam Hemsworth)—she gradually comes to trust in her ability to forge discerning relationships. Wary of revealing her vulnerability, she first befriends District 11 Tribute Rue, a young girl who serves as her substitute sister as the two form a strong female alliance. As the series progresses, Katniss gains more allies, wins over the public, and changes her whole world for the better.

Katniss's relationship with her fellow District 12 Tribute, friend, "star-crossed lover," and eventual husband, Peeta (Josh Hutcherson), is in many ways a reversal of expected gender roles. Peeta often expresses more emotional sensitivity and is more relationship-driven than Katniss. Her physical prowess typically exceeds his (*she* saves *his* life), and they are approximately the same height (why does the guy always have to be taller, anyway?).

Though the final film's epilogue paints a glowing picture of Katniss as the perfect little housewife cuddling her baby, the books make it clear that it took her years to comply with Peeta's wish to have children. Whether teenage warrior or wife and mother, Katniss does everything her own way, guided by her own moral compass. May the odds be ever in her favor.

Did You Know?

Lawrence initially feared she was too old and too blonde for the role of sixteen-year-old Katniss. "I talked to Suzanne after I got the part," she said in 2012. "Hearing 'I know you can do it' from the woman who created Katniss herself, I feel like a huge weight had been lifted off my shoulders. That gave me the boost that I needed."

Josh Hutcherson and Jennifer Lawrence

Super-heroines

It started on television. Catwomen Eartha Kitt and Julie Newmar made *purrfect* foils for Batman in the 1960s series. In the 1970s, Lynda Carter fought for justice as *Wonder Woman*, followed by Lindsay Wagner in *The Bionic Woman*. It wasn't until later that the movie industry caught on, eventually giving us a slew of empowered female crusaders. From girls with above-average skills to superwomen boasting magical powers, these characters inspire us all with their awesome abilities.

Carrie Fisher

AS "PRINCESS LEIA ORGANA"

The Star Wars series (1977–)

When you're the only girl in the entire galaxy, you've got a lot to prove.

As Princess Leia Organa (née Skywalker) in the most popular space saga of all time, Carrie Fisher proved her worth, from the first film to her appearances in the latter-day sequels. Though creator George Lucas made his heroes male, his villains male, and his Wookiee and droids male (can a robot even *have* a gender?), he wrote his one female lead as a Force-ful, gutsy, no-nonsense broad. It was one small step for princesses, one giant leap for women in outer space.

Nineteen when she was cast, Fisher brought an uncommon surplus of smarts and spunk to the role—even editing her dialogue (later using her skills to become a best-selling writer and in-demand script doctor) and infusing the character with her own sweet-tart personality. Lucas had auditioned "thousands of people" before finding Fisher, who was an actual princess, in a sense, being the child of Hollywood royalty (Debbie Reynolds and Eddie Fisher). "It was finding somebody who could hold her own against strong actors," Lucas remembered, "and still be the authority figure that she needed to be."

The daughter of Padmé Amidala (played by Natalie Portman in the prequels) and Anakin Skywalker, Leia was raised far from her twin, Luke (Mark Hamill), on the planet of Alderaan. First valiantly striking out to oppose the Empire as a senator and then to fight with the Rebel Alliance, Leia later starts the Resistance to defy the First Order.

Before *Star Wars* soared into theaters in 1977, fairy-tale princesses were a predictable lot, invariably beautiful, passive, and frightened. In her introductory scene, Leia is in need of help, but she's far from helpless. As Fisher observed, she's more of a "distressing damsel" than a damsel in distress. When Luke and Han Solo (Harrison Ford) arrive on the Death Star to rescue her, the guys falter on their getaway plan. Instead of waiting uselessly in the wings, she grabs Luke's blaster, shoots a hole in the wall, and quips to Han, "Into the

Carrie Fisher as Princess Leia in *Star Wars Episode IV: A New Hope* garbage chute, fly boy!" Her explanation? *Somebody* had to save our skins." Even as they fall in love, Leia brooks none of Han's condescending attitude; she grows fond of the arrogant star pilot in spite of his machismo, not because of it.

⟡

"Listen, I don't know who you are or where you came from, but from now on, you'll do as I tell you. Okay?"

—"PRINCESS LEIA"

⟡

The second part of the saga was coscripted by Leigh Brackett, a respected sci-fi author and veteran Hollywood screenwriter known for her work on *The Big Sleep* (1946), among other classics. In *The Empire Strikes Back* (1980), Leia trades in her flowing white robes (regal, but so easy to trip over) for sensible slacks, and her trademark buns for practical braids as her role shifts from princess and senator to rebel leader. She lays out battle plans, briefs the pilots on their missions, and has replaced her haughty demeanor with self-assured authority. She uses the Force to sense when Luke is getting smacked down by Darth Vader, and commands Lando (Billy Dee Williams) to turn the *Millennium Falcon* around and rescue her brother.

Leia once again plays rescuer in *Return of the Jedi* (1983), saving Han in Jabba the Hutt's palace—though, of course, she gets captured and enslaved by the sadistic slug. "When [Lucas] showed me the outfit, I thought he was kidding," Fisher said of the infamous metal bikini she sports. "What redeems it is I get to kill him, which was so enjoyable," the actress recalled. "I sawed his neck off with that chain. . . . I really relished that because I hated wearing that outfit." Rather than holding out for a hero, she saves herself by strangling Jabba with

Leia aims at a stormtrooper.

Carrie Fisher and Harrison Ford in *Return of the Jedi*

the very chain that shackles her, turning her exploitational ensemble into a symbol of empowerment.

It's a pity that Leia only taps into the Force to sense when Luke is in trouble, because she might have made a daunting warrior if she'd ever been handed a light-saber. "Even in space," Carrie Fisher told Stephen Colbert shortly before her death in 2016, "for women, there's a double stan-dard." She may not be a Jedi Knight, but she finally fulfills her potential as General Leia Organa in *Star Wars: The Force Awak-ens* (2015) and *The Last Jedi* (2017).

These days, there are feisty females aplenty in contemporary fantasy, adventure, and sci-fi movies, but they all owe a debt to Princess Leia. Without her example, we may have never seen the likes of Ellen Ripley, Sarah Connor, Belle in *Beauty and the Beast,* Hermione Granger, Elsa in *Frozen,* or Moana—and the list goes on. The Force will be with her, always.

Did You Know?

In a 1983 interview with *Rolling Stone,* Carrie Fisher admitted that she used to feel guilty about her fame and good fortune. "I finally quit apologizing for it," she said. "For being something different. For being strong. Strength is a style."

Zhang Ziyi

AS "JEN YU"

Crouching Tiger, Hidden Dragon (2000)

Pre-dating American movies like *Kill Bill* (2003) and *Wonder Woman* (2017) was an epic Chinese martial-arts film featuring not one, but three seriously spectacular female fighters. Ang Lee's Oscar-winning 2000 masterpiece *Crouching Tiger, Hidden Dragon* is many things: action, drama, romance, fantasy, period piece, and feminist film. Though Asian-cinema superstar Chow Yun-fat gets top billing, he—along with the other men—is essentially a supporting character in a story about women.

Set in China's Qing Dynasty in the early 1800s, *Crouching Tiger* explores the theme of repressed power. All three of the story's primary ladies have been denied rights because of their gender, yet each reacts in a different way. Skilled warrior Yu Shu Lien (Michelle Yeoh) is noble and restrained, with a disciplined inner strength that she uses for good. The sinister Jade Fox (Cheng Pei-pei) has turned to the dark side in revolt against the unfair treatment she has received. Nineteen-year-old Chinese sensation Zhang Ziyi played Jen Yu, a headstrong fireball torn between the two older women, between good and evil.

By day, Jen is a governor's daughter betrothed to a wealthy man. By night, she's secretly a savage swordswoman. Clad in black like a ninja, she soars over rooftops to steal an ancient sword known as the Green Destiny, which she describes as "beautiful but dangerous," a fitting description of herself as well. Jen's bottled rage over her arranged marriage is unleashed in her explosive fight scenes; she spins, flips, defies gravity, and wounds her opponents with a poetic brutality. The movie abounds with breathtaking visuals, including a battle in the Gobi Desert and a lyrical swordfight on the high branches of bamboo trees. The most impressive fight sequence may be when Jen takes on a band of male warriors in a restaurant, destroying half the property in the process. She teaches a man called Iron Arm a lesson with one hand, while sipping her tea with the other, proclaiming, "I am the Invincible Sword Goddess!"

Jen is proud, determined, and absolutely unwilling to be dominated by anyone. She bruises a lot of ribs just to retrieve a hair

Zhang Ziyi as Jen Yu in *Crouching Tiger, Hidden Dragon*

A fight scene with Zhang Ziyi and Michelle Yeoh

"I am the Invincible Sword Goddess, armed with the incredible Green Destiny. Be you Li or Southern Crane, lower your head and ask for mercy!"

—"JEN YU"

comb swiped by a bandit (Chang Chen), who later becomes the love of her life. This young woman has the power to slay an entire army, yet even she is a slave to tradition; she must marry the man selected by her family or bring shame upon them for generations. Faced with an impossible decision, in the end, Jen Yu pulls a *Thelma & Louise* in order to remain free.

A delicate balance of heart-pounding intensity and quiet restraint, the film is reminiscent of *Sense and Sensibility* (1995), Ang Lee's Jane Austen adaptation (scripted by Emma Thompson) about women coping

with a society that represses their aspirations. Traditionally, Chinese culture places more value on boys than girls at birth, but *Crouching Tiger, Hidden Dragon* flips that custom on its head by honoring strong women—and even trying to understand the villainous Jade Fox, who explains the double standard that led to her ruin: "Your master underestimated us women," she says to her male foe. "Sure, he'd sleep with me, but he would never teach me. He deserved to die by a woman's hand!"

Lee always dreamed of making a martial-arts movie, but spent years searching for the right material. He finally found it in an obscure novel from the late 1930s. "This is a very male-dominant genre, and I suspect the woman warrior is a male fantasy," the director told *Films in Review*. "But this book is one of the rare cases where we take the emotional tour with the women. We take their point of view, and they get to carry the story."

Hollywood has a history of portraying Chinese women as stereotypically docile girlfriends or wives. *Crouching Tiger* demolished those clichés and became an international mainstream hit, though it initiated few radical changes in the West. "After *Crouching Tiger*," Zhang Ziyi revealed, "I got a lot of offers [in Hollywood], but I turned them down because they were all victim roles." A major star in the East, Ziyi is best known stateside for *Memoirs of a Geisha* (2005) and *Godzilla, King of the Monsters* (2019).

Did You Know?

According to Michelle Yeoh, the film's title refers to hidden strength. "If it's said in Chinese," she explained in 2000, "what it really means is on a mountain, you know, where tigers look like they are down and they're quiet, it doesn't mean that they don't have the ability to be fierce."

Jen takes on an army of warriors single-handedly.

Emma Watson

AS "HERMIONE GRANGER"

The Harry Potter films (2001–2011)

Harry Potter and His Incredibly Brilliant Friend Hermione

Granger, Who Saves Him with Her Knowledge Time and Again. If there were any justice in the world, at least one of the seven novels and eight films in the Harry Potter franchise would bear this title. We all know that the boy wizard owes much of his success to Hermione, even Harry himself, who admits that he's "not as good" at magic as she is.

In *Harry Potter and the Sorcerer's Stone* (2001), eleven-year-old Emma Watson first embodied the bossy, know-it-all witch who befriends Harry (Daniel Radcliffe) and Ron (Rupert Grint)—though the boys are far from charmed when they meet her aboard the Hogwarts Express. "Is that a real spell?" she scoffs at Ron's feeble attempt at magic. "It's not very good, is it?" With these words, her place in the Potterverse is firmly established: she's smarter than everyone else, and not afraid to own it. Though the Sorting Hat contemplates putting her in Ravenclaw (where cleverness prevails), luckily for Harry, she's sorted into Gryffindor, home of the brave. It is Hermione's combination of brains and bravery that makes her an essential ingredient in Harry's ability to escape danger and ultimately defeat the evil Lord Voldemort.

J.K. Rowling based Hermione loosely upon herself, a former top student whose intelligence, imagination, and ingenuity jettisoned her from struggling single mom to the world's first billionaire book author. Hermione's heroism was deliberate on Rowling's part. "You don't see a lot of Hermiones in film or on TV except to be laughed at," she said in 2014. "I mean that the intense, clever, in some ways not terribly self-aware, girl is rarely the heroine, and I really wanted her to be the heroine."

Founded by a gender-balanced quartet (two men, two women) and boasting a co-ed Quidditch team, Hogwarts School of Witchcraft and Wizardry was clearly intended by its author to be an equal-opportunity environment. Still, the dominant characters are male, which makes Hermione all the more important as the key female, resident brainiac, and loyal friend. "Hermione was the one that stuck with Harry all the way through that last installment, that very last part of the adventure. It wasn't Ron," Rowling observed in a 2014 discussion with Emma Watson.

Emma Watson as Hermione Granger in *Harry Potter and the Deathly Hallows*

As the series progresses, Harry and Ron grow so reliant on Hermione that they would be lost without her. In their second adventure, she brews the complicated Polyjuice Potion, breaking "about fifty school rules" in the process, and—when even the teachers are unable to catch the monster endangering the students—Hermione solves the mystery single-handedly. But it's in the third film, *Harry Potter and the Prisoner of Azkaban* (2004), that a now teenaged Hermione comes into her own. Superman-like, she turns back time to save the lives of Sirius Black and Buckbeak, making her this movie's hero. What's more, she lets go and punches "foul, loathsome, evil little cockroach" Draco Malfoy (Tom Felton) right in the face, momentarily discarding her wand and spell books for an old-fashioned right hook. "That felt good," she sighs as Malfoy cowers in fear.

Because Hermione is Muggle-born and knows how it feels to be an outsider, she has a soft spot for the underprivileged (like Dobby the house elf). She also stands up to tyrannical Dolores Umbridge, organizes Dumbledore's Army, and, by the penultimate movie, has stepped up to being the head of the trio. In their final adventure, she is Ron's shining star and Harry's guide in his quest for the Deathly Hallows, serving as the brains of the whole operation. As Watson explained in 2017, "Hermione finds a way to wield her intelligence and become really the leader in this group of two other boys, and that's kind of the role that she assumes." Harry may get the glory, but "Hermione is the one with the plan," Watson said. "She's in control."

After graduating from Hogwarts in films, Watson went on to earn a degree in English literature from Brown University and to use her voice as an advocate for the empowerment of women. Having played both Hermione and the progressive Disney heroine Belle in the 2017 live-action *Beauty and the Beast*, Watson has inspired a generation of girls to use their minds and save the day.

Did You Know?

Emma Watson was made a United Nations Goodwill Ambassador in 2014, the same year she launched the HeForShe campaign to involve men in issues of gender equality. In 2015, she appeared on *Time* magazine's list of the world's most influential people.

Rupert Grint, Daniel Radcliffe, and Emma Watson

> "Actually, I'm highly logical, which allows me to look past extraneous detail and perceive clearly that which others overlook."
> —"HERMIONE GRANGER"

Hermione brews the Polyjuice Potion in *Harry Potter and the Chamber of Secrets*.

Uma Thurman
AS "THE BRIDE, A.K.A. BLACK MAMBA, A.K.A. BEATRIX KIDDO"

Kill Bill, volumes i and ii (2003-2004)

On the set of *Pulp Fiction* in 1994, writer/director Quentin Tarantino and actress Uma Thurman started plotting a movie they hoped to make. As they spun ideas and swapped concepts, a character took shape called "the Bride," a former paid assassin seeking revenge on the hit squad that killed her groom (and tried their best to kill her) before her wedding. For Thurman, it meant a dream role; for Tarantino, his big chance to do Hong Kong–style cinema his way. In 2003, their collaboration yielded a masterful mélange of action, exploitation, and martial arts, laced with Tarantino's signature dark humor.

The first volume of the epic is a violent Japanese Manga comic come to life. With only the faintest glimmer of life still surging through her body, Thurman's bloody Bride becomes a one-woman army hell-bent on a single objective: vengeance. After bashing in the head of a horrid hospital rapist who calls her the p-word once too often, she begins methodically crossing off her list those who have crossed her: two men (David Carradine and Michael Madsen) and three legitimately ferocious ladies played by Vivica A. Fox, Daryl Hannah, and Lucy Liu as a crime boss supported by an impressive network of female badassery.

Armed with the world's finest Hattori Hanzo sword, our blonde killing machine dons her iconic yellow tracksuit, zips up her motorcycle jacket, and heads to Tokyo, where she out-ninjas dozens of sword-wielding bodyguards all by her lonesome. Not since the days of Pam Grier has a woman been given such free reign as a deadly force in cinema. Hacking off limbs with wild abandon, the Bride spares a wet-behind-the-ears Yakuza (Japanese mafia) wannabe, spanking him with her weapon and ordering, "Go home to your mother!"

Beaten, brutalized, and buried alive, this head-severin', eyeball-pluckin' mama rises from the grave once again in the second installment. If she wasn't angry enough before, she's now as mad as a flaming hornet's nest. After Daryl Hannah's Elle mercifully kills off a man who has just insulted the intelligence of blonde

Uma Thurman as the Bride in *Kill Bill*

Uma Thurman and Chiaki Kuriyama

women (never do this in front of a blonde woman), she too gets her comeuppance at the hands of the Bride. The last on the list is Bill, who appeals to her feminine nature, trying to soften her by tugging at her maternal heartstrings. But it does little good in the end.

Tarantino has described *Kill Bill* as "a feminist statement," and—though some have argued that it's merely hyper-masculine violence disguised as feminism—its mega-powerful females dominate the movie and the men, and they don't show a lot of skin while they're at it. Never a scantily clad sex object, Thurman wears androgynous yellow (neither girlish pink nor boyish blue) to make her gender less of a focal point. Even the title has a feminist connotation, implying that Bill, the patriarchal ruler of the Deadly Vipers, must be eliminated in order for the leading lady to be free.

Thurman plays Beatrix Kiddo with a restrained fury that runs unfathomably deep, her imposing stature (5'11") and the defiant set of her jaw working in her favor as she grounds the larger-than-life character

with an aura of authenticity. The rage she expresses as the Bride was rivaled by Uma's real-life anger over the difficulty she faced during filmmaking, an experience she later referred to as "dehumanization to the point of death." In 2018, Thurman accused Tarantino of pressuring her to drive a stunt car that crashed—resulting in chronically painful injuries—and accused the film's male producers, including Harvey Weinstein and Lawrence Bender, of covering up the incident. (Honestly, hadn't these guys seen the movie? You don't mess with Uma!)

Tarantino later apologized, and Thurman accepted, but the frustration the performer felt toward the Hollywood system has lingered. "When they turned on me after the accident," she told the *New York Times*, "I went from being a creative contributor and performer to being like a broken tool." Yet, in the wake of scandals and bitter feelings, *Kill Bill*'s legacy as a blood-splattered feminist tirade remains. Many women have told Thurman "that the film helped them in their lives, whether they were feeling oppressed or struggling or had a bad boyfriend or felt badly about themselves, that that film released in them some survival energy that was helpful."

Did You Know?

Three months after giving birth, Thurman undertook an Olympian training regimen to get her body into shape for the film. She next had to learn Kung Fu, swordplay, wire work, stunts, and a smattering of Japanese and Chinese languages.

"When I woke up, I went on what the movie advertisements refer to as a roaring rampage of revenge. I roared and I rampaged, and I got bloody satisfaction."

—"THE BRIDE"

Top: Daryl Hannah, Vivica A. Fox, Michael Madsen, and Lucy Liu as the Deadly Vipers. Bottom: Quentin Tarantino directs Uma Thurman.

Charlize Theron
AS "IMPERATOR FURIOSA"

Mad Max: Fury Road (2015)

Since the 1979 release of George Miller's low-budget action classic *Mad Max,* the franchise has become a high-octane cult favorite, particularly with male audiences. Macho Mel Gibson embodied the post-apocalyptic antihero in the first three movies. In the third, *Beyond Thunderdome* (1985), Gibson gained a formidable African American woman as his costar: Tina Turner as the villainous Aunty Entity.

Thirty years later, Miller brought women to the forefront in his fourth entry, *Fury Road,* starring Tom Hardy as Max and Charlize Theron as the lionhearted Imperator Furiosa. A truck driver instead of a glamour girl, Theron trades her lipstick and platinum locks for a soot-coated forehead and a buzz cut; a mechanical left arm gives her the look of a souped-up warrior. While not technically a superhero (she has no special powers besides courage), she embodies all the traits of a superstar action hero, picking up where Ellen Ripley and Sarah Connor left off.

Operating an armored truck called the War Rig for the barbaric ruler Immortan Joe (Hugh Keays-Byrne), Furiosa flees the Citadel with Joe's five wives in search of green land, only to discover it's turned just as water-starved as everyplace else. The scene in which Max is attacked by this band of babes in the barren desert is reminiscent of Russ Meyer's 1965 ode to violent women, *Faster, Pussycat! Kill! Kill!*—except, in this case, the gals are not murderous go-go dancers, but human beings fed up with their enslavement by a man who uses young, beautiful women as his "breeding stock." The men, Max and Nux (played by Nicholas Hoult), and women reluctantly grow to trust each other as they realize they're on the same side and must work together to find redemption.

Retaining the flavor of the original films—a minimum of dialogue, a maximum of driving, and a lot of dust—Miller crafts something new and forward thinking: a reboot that reflects the subtle shifts toward a more inclusive Hollywood that were starting to happen at the time. In the three decades since his last *Mad Max* adventure, Miller admitted, "I've gone from being very male-dominant to being surrounded by magnificent women. I can't help but be a feminist." The writer/director

Charlize Theron as Imperator Furiosa in *Mad Max: Fury Road*

hired his wife, Margaret Sixel, to edit the film. "She had never cut an action movie," Miller recalled, "and she said, 'Why on earth would you want me to cut the movie?' and I said, 'Because if it were the usual kind of guys, it would look like every other action movie you see.'"

There is a certain poetry and dignity in this kamikrazee adrenaline fest. A woman of few words, Furiosa's actions define her.

———◇———

"Out here, everything hurts. You want to get through this? Do as I say. Now pick up what you can and run."

—"FURIOSA"

———◇———

With her Spiderman-quick reflexes, she saves Max's life when he falls from the rig, a gesture that he later repays by reviving her with his blood when she's dying. Furiosa and Max both become saviors of their world, a happy ending that the filmmakers shared when *Fury Road* became one of the year's most acclaimed films and an Oscar nominee for Best Picture.

When Charlize Theron first heard rumors that a female lead would be cast in *Fury Road*, she was skeptical. "I've heard that before," she told *Elle* in 2015, "and then I'm going to be the chick that ends up in the back of the frame with the push-up bra and with a wisp of hair in my mouth." But when she met Miller, "I believed him." This filmmaker, she noted, understood that "women are just eager to feel like they're on an equal playing field. I don't want to be put on a pedestal. I don't want to be anything other than who we are." Using this simple concept, Miller and Theron created an authentically strong, flawed, and admirable woman in Furiosa.

Starting as a dancer in her native South Africa, Theron branched out into acting after being sidelined by a knee injury. As she gained experience, she challenged herself with edgier material, eventually winning an Oscar for her daring portrayal of serial killer Aileen Wuornos in Patty Jenkins's *Monster* (2003). Since then, she has continued to defy Hollywood's expectations, following Furiosa with cyberterrorist Cipher in *The Fate of the Furious* (2017) and ass-kicking spy Lorraine Broughton in *Atomic Blonde* (2017). Theron has also started her own production company in order to create more high-quality roles for women.

Did You Know?

The close-shaved cut Theron sports in the film was her own idea, and she was liberated by the experience. "It's unbelievable how much time we spend on our hair," she observed. "I emptied two garbage bags full of hair products and brushes. There's something very freeing in that."

Top: Tom Hardy and Charlize Theron. Bottom: Charlize Theron

Gal Gadot

AS "DIANA PRINCE"

Wonder Woman (2017)

It certainly took Hollywood long enough to bring Wonder

Woman to the big screen, considering she first appeared in comic-book form in 1941. But, at last, director Patty Jenkins did justice to the iconic Amazon, giving her a proper tribute in 2017's *Wonder Woman*, starring Gal Gadot as the ultimate dynamic dame, Princess Diana of Themyscira (alias: Diana Prince). Taking some inspiration from Richard Donner's classic *Superman* (1978), Jenkins delivered a fun yet earnest paean for truth, justice, and the goodness inherent in humanity.

Wonder Woman is the creation of psychologist, feminist, and inventor of the lie-detector test William Moulton Marston, a man who saw the need for a female superhero as World War II loomed. "Not even girls want to be girls," he once said, "so long as our feminine archetype lacks force, strength, and power." He believed his character to be the ideal mixture of feminine beauty and warmth, and masculine brawn. With her Lasso of Truth, her shield, and her Bracelets of Submission, the DC Comics heroine has since become a cultural touchstone.

On TV, Lynda Carter broke ground as a glorious Wonder Woman in the late 1970s. Though the series had a campy tone ("In your satin tights/Fighting for your rights," the theme song warbled), Carter upheld Diana's dignity, becoming a beloved embodiment of female empowerment. The concept for a big-screen version was bandied around Hollywood to no avail, until Gadot first leapt into action in 2016's *Batman v. Superman: Dawn of Justice*, all but stealing the movie out from under Ben Affleck and Henry Cavill. It was time for a solo film, one directed by a woman who had lobbied for years to bring Wonder Woman to life after helming the Oscar-winning *Monster* in 2003.

Patty Jenkins was conscious of Wonder Woman's seventy-five-year legacy as a feminist emblem, but was more concerned with making an entertaining film. "I have always wanted to be last-wave feminism," Jenkins told *Variety*, "where you're so feminist, you're not thinking about it at all. Where you're like, 'Of course this super-

Gal Gadot as Diana Prince in *Wonder Woman*

Patty Jenkins directs Gal Gadot on location in Italy.

"Only love can save this world. So I stay. I fight, and I give, for the world I know can be. This is my mission. Now. Forever."

—"WONDER WOMAN"

hero is the greatest superhero of all time. Oh, she's a woman? I wasn't even thinking about that.'" Her movie hits the mark, tempering Diana's nobility and fighting skills with screwball-comedy banter between Diana and Chris Pine's charming spy Steve Trevor, who becomes her ally after initially doubting her abilities. She can't stop World War I, he says, but they should "get back to London and try to get the men who can." Little does he know. "I'm the man who can," she assures him.

Steve and his merry band of misfits are heroic, resourceful men, which is helpful; this goddess wouldn't get very far sur-rounded by a bunch of weaklings. Taking nothing away from the guys, Wonder Woman rescues the human race, while her love interest does a gender-role reversal and becomes the self-sacrificing character. "I can save today," he realizes, "you can save the world!"

From lush Themyscira Island—where Diana leaves her aunt, Antiope (Robin Wright), and her mother, Hippolyta (Connie Nielsen)—to the grim European battlefields, indelible imagery dominates the film: Diana marches through no-man's-land in slow motion, deflecting a hail of gunfire; she soars into the air with her glowing lasso and drives a sword into General Ludendorff; she conquers Ares with her bracelets as flames glint off her head-dress and electric currents flow through her forearms. A true cinematic hero is born.

After training for combat and serving two years in the Israel Defense Forces, Gal Gadot was eager to portray a superwoman. "I love everything Wonder Woman represents," the actress told a reporter in 2016. "She's all about love and compassion and truth and justice and equality, and she's a whole lot of woman." So much greatness can wear a girl down, so Gadot gave her "this attitude," she said. "I wanted her to have a smirk."

By late 2017, *Wonder Woman* had officially become the highest-grossing super-hero origin film of all time, proving that comic-book movies with female leads (and with female directors) can strike box-office gold. "It may have taken four films to get there," *Variety*'s review declared, "but the DC Extended Universe has finally produced a good old-fashioned superhero." Its success led to a sequel, *Wonder Woman 1984* (2019), featuring Kristen Wiig as Cheetah and Gadot once again saving mankind—even though we don't deserve her.

Did You Know?

In 2016, Wonder Woman was made a United Nations Honorary Ambassador for the Empowerment of Women and Girls, then was withdrawn after protestors claimed she was too sexualized. "They say, 'If she's smart and strong, she can't also be sexy.' That's not fair," Gal Gadot said in response to the controversy. "Why can't she be all of the above?"

Chris Pine and Gal Gadot

More
Dynamic Dames

More Pre-Code Bad Girls

Joan Crawford as "Marian Martin" in *Possessed* (1931)

Kay Francis as "Madame Mariette Colet" in *Trouble in Paradise* (1932)

Jean Harlow as "Lil Andrews" in *Red-Headed Woman* (1932)

Miriam Hopkins as "Gilda Farrell" in *Design for Living* (1933)

Joan Blondell as "Blondie Johnson" in *Blondie Johnson* (1933)

Claudette Colbert as "Sally Trent" in *Torch Singer* (1933)

Aline McMahon as "Olga" in *Heat Lightning* (1934)

More Reel Role Models

Maria Falconetti as "Joan of Arc" in *The Passion of Joan of Arc* (1928)

Greer Garson as "Marie Curie" in *Madame Curie* (1943)

Sally Field as "Norma Rae Wilson" in *Norma Rae* (1979)

Sissy Spacek as "Loretta Lynn" in *Coal Miner's Daughter* (1980)

Madonna as "Eva Perón" in *Evita* (1996)

Kristen Stewart as "Joan Jett" in *The Runaways* (2010)

Taraji P. Henson as "Katherine Johnson" in *Hidden Figures* (2016)

More Big Bad Mamas

Maureen O'Hara as "Doris Walker" in *Miracle on 34th Street* (1947)

Juanita Moore as "Annie Johnson" in *Imitation of Life* (1959)

Cicely Tyson as "Rebecca Morgan" in *Sounder* (1972)

Ellen Burstyn as "Alice Hyatt" in *Alice Doesn't Live Here Anymore* (1974)

Cher as "Rusty Dennis" in *Mask* (1983)

Kathy Bates as "Dolores Claiborne" in *Dolores Claiborne* (1995)

Frances McDormand as "Mildred Hayes" in *Three Billboards Outside Ebbing, Missouri* (2017)

More Fatal Femmes

Loretta Young as "Mary Martin" in *Midnight Mary* (1933)

Maria Montez as "Naja" in *Cobra Woman* (1944)

Lana Turner as "Cora Smith" in *The Postman Always Rings Twice* (1946)

Gloria Grahame as "Debby Marsh" in *The Big Heat* (1953)

Susan Hayward as "Barbara Graham" in *I Want to Live!* (1959)

Faye Dunaway as "Bonnie Parker" in *Bonnie and Clyde* (1967)

Renée Zellweger as "Roxy Hart" in *Chicago* (2002)

More Ladies Who Laugh

Judy Garland as "Susan Bradley" in *The Harvey Girls* (1946)

Judy Holliday as "Billie Dawn" in *Born Yesterday* (1950)

Lily Tomlin as "Violet Newstead," Jane Fonda as "Judy Bernly," and Dolly Parton as "Dorelee Rhodes" in *9 to 5* (1980)

Kathleen Turner as "Joan Wilder" in *Romancing the Stone* (1984)

Ricki Lake as "Tracy Turnblad" in *Hairspray* (1988)

Reese Witherspoon as "Elle Woods" in *Legally Blonde* (2001)

Parminder Nagra as "Jess Bhamra" in *Bend It Like Beckham* (2002)

More Women of Mystery

Veronica Lake as "Janet Henry" in *The Glass Key* (1942)

Ella Raines as "Kansas" in *Phantom Lady* (1944)

Lucille Ball as "Sandra Carpenter" in *Lured* (1947)

Lauren Bacall as "Nora Temple" in *Key Largo* (1948)

Glenn Close as "Teddy Barnes" in *Jagged Edge* (1985)

Ashley Judd as "Libby Parsons" in *Double Jeopardy* (1999)

Rooney Mara as "Lisbeth Salander" in *The Girl with the Dragon Tattoo* (2011)

More Strong Survivors

Jean Arthur as "Phoebe Titus" in *Arizona* (1940)

Debbie Reynolds as "Molly Brown" in *The Unsinkable Molly Brown* (1964)

Diane Lane as "Corrine Burns" in *Ladies and Gentlemen, the Fabulous Stains* (1982)

Farrah Fawcett as "Marjorie" in *Extremities* (1986)

Mary Stuart Masterson as "Idgie Threadgoode" in *Fried Green Tomatoes* (1991)

Demi Moore as "Jordan O'Neil" in *G.I. Jane* (1997)

Gabourey Sidibe as "Precious" in *Precious* (2009)

More Superheroines

Drew Barrymore as "Charlie McGee" in *Firestarter* (1984)

Michelle Pfeiffer as "Selina Kyle, a.k.a. Catwoman" in *Batman Returns* (1992)

Halle Berry as "Storm" in the *X-Men* films (2000-2014)

Angelina Jolie as "Lara Croft" in *Lara Croft: Tomb Raider* (2001) and *Tomb Raider: Cradle of Life* (2003)

Milla Jovovich as "Alice" in the *Resident Evil* series (2002-2016)

Scarlett Johansson as "Natasha Romanoff, a.k.a. Black Widow" in the *Iron Man* and *Avengers* films (2010-2019)

Idina Menzel as the voice of "Queen Elsa" in *Frozen* (2013)

Bibliography

Books

Abbott, Karen. *American Rose: A Nation Laid Bare: The Life and Times of Gypsy Rose Lee.* New York: Random House, 2010.

Acker, Ally. *Reel Women: Pioneers of the Cinema.* New York: Continuum, 1991.

Bach, Steven. *Marlene Dietrich: Life and Legend.* New York: William Morrow, 1992.

Basinger, Jeanine. *A Woman's View.* New York: Alfred A. Knopf, 1995.

Biesen, Sheri Chinen. *Blackout: World War II and the Origins of Film Noir.* Baltimore, MD: Johns Hopkins University Press, 2005.

Capua, Michelangelo. *Jean Negulesco: The Life and Films.* Jefferson, NC: McFarland & Co., 2017.

Carman, Emily. *Independent Stardom: Freelance Women in the Hollywood Studio System.* Austin: University of Texas Press, 2016.

Chandler, Charlotte. *Ingrid: Ingrid Bergman, a Personal Biography.* New York: Applause, 2007.

———. *She Always Knew How: Mae West, a Personal Biography.* New York: Simon and Schuster, 2009.

Daniel, Douglass K. *Anne Bancroft: A Life.* Lexington, KY: University Press of Kentucky, 2017.

Edwards, Anne. *Vivien Leigh: A Biography.* New York: Simon and Schuster, 1977.

Grier, Pam, with Andrea Cagan. *Foxy: My Life in Three Acts.* New York: Hachette, 2010.

Haskell, Molly. *Frankly, My Dear: Gone with the Wind Revisited.* New Haven, CT: Yale University Press, 2009.

Hawn, Goldie, with Wendy Holden. *A Lotus Grows in the Mud.* New York: Penguin, 2005.

Jorgensen, Jay, and Manoah Bowman. *Grace Kelly: Hollywood Dream Girl.* New York: Dey St., 2017.

LaSalle, Mick. *Complicated Women.* New York: Thomas Dunne Books, 2000.

Loren, Sophia. *Yesterday, Today, Tomorrow: My Life.* New York: Atria, 2014.

Loy, Myrna. *Being and Becoming.* New York: Primus, 1987.

Mair, George. *Oprah Winfrey: The Real Story.* Secaucus, NJ: Carol Publishing Group, 1998.

McCarthy, Todd. *Howard Hawks: The Grey Fox of Hollywood.* New York: Grove Press, 1997.

Rehak, Melanie. *Girl Sleuth: Nancy Drew and the Women Who Created Her.* Orlando, FL: Harcourt, 2005.

Schickel, Richard. *The Stars.* New York: Bonanza Books, 1962.

Sikov, Ed. *Dark Victory: The Life of Bette Davis.* New York: Henry Holt, 2007.

Sragow, Michael. *Victor Fleming: An American Movie Master.* Lexington, KY: University Press of Kentucky, 2013.

Stenn, David. *Clara Bow: Runnin' Wild.* New York: Doubleday, 1988.

Tapert, Annette. *The Power of Glamour.* New York: Crown, 1998.

Taymor, Julie, and Clancy Sigal. *Frida: Bringing Frida Kahlo's Life and Art to Film.* Edited by Linda Sunshine. New York: Newmarket, 2002.

The Editors of *People. The 100 Best Celebrity Photos.* New York: Time, Inc., 2017.

Tierney, Gene, with Mickey Herskowitz. *Self-Portrait.* New York: Simon and Schuster, 1979.

Turner, Tina, with Kurt Loder. *I, Tina: My Life Story.* New York: William Morrow, 1986.

Vieira, Mark A. *Greta Garbo: A Cinematic Legacy.* New York: Harry N. Abrams, 2005.

Watts, Jill. *Mae West: An Icon in Black and White.* Oxford: Oxford University Press, 2003.

Wills, David. *Audrey: The 50s.* New York: Dey St., 2016.

Wilson, Victoria. *A Life of Barbara Stanwyck.* New York: Simon and Schuster, 2013.

Wood, Ean. *The Josephine Baker Story.* London: Sanctuary, 2000.

Zinnemann, Fred. *A Life in the Movies.* New York: Charles Scribner's Sons, 1992.

Articles

Babb, Francesca. "Nancy Meyers: The Rom-Com Queen." *The Independent*, January 9, 2010.

Benjamin, George. "The Return of Roz." *Modern Screen*, January 1940.

Caldwell, Carol. "Carrie Fisher: A Few Words on Princess Leia, Fame, and Feminism." *Rolling Stone*, July 21, 1983.

Canfield, Alyce. "Life Begins for Hedy Lamarr." *Screenland*, August 1946.

Dowd, Maureen. "Opinion: This Is Why Uma Thurman Is Angry." *New York Times*, February 3, 2018.

Finke, Nikki. "A Working Girl Makes Good." *Los Angeles Times*, December 17, 1988.

Garrett, Lou Ann. "Hedy's Secret Weapon." *Motion Picture*, November 1944.

Hall, Gladys. "Norma Shearer Tells What a 'Free Soul' Really Means." *Motion Picture*, April 1932.

Hayek, Salma. "Opinion: Harvey Weinstein Is My Monster Too." *New York Times*, December 13, 2017.

Kamp, David. "When Liz Met Dick." *Vanity Fair*, March 1998.

Knoedelseder Jr., William K. "'*Alien*'s Sigourney Weaver: The Hero Is a Woman." *Los Angeles Times*, June 4, 1979.

Lauterbach, Richard E. "Close Up: Gypsy Rose Lee." *Life*, December 14, 1942.

Lloyd, Mary Anne. "Sigourney: The Star Find of '79 Defends Her Semi-Strip in *Alien*." *Photoplay*, December 1979.

Milstein, Fredric. "Movie Reviews: Coffy Out to Get White Mafiosi." *Los Angeles Times*, June 15, 1973.

"On the 'Bright Road' of 'Carmen' and 'Joe.'" *New York Times*, October 24, 1954.

Tuckman, Joe. "That Frida Feeling." *The Guardian*, August 30, 2001.

Walker, Michael. "Tina Turner's Story Through a Disney Prism." *Los Angeles Times*, May 16, 1993.

Weller, Sheila. "The Ride of a Lifetime." *Vanity Fair*, March 2011.

Wilson, Elizabeth. "The New Sophisticate of the Screen." *Screenland*, November 1934.

Woerner, Meredith. "Superhero Showdown: Anything They Can Do She Can Do, Except Backward and in Heels." *Los Angeles Times*, March 24, 2016.

Online Articles

Anthony, Carl Sferrazza. "She Was No Angel, Thank Goodness." *Washington Post,*
August 17, 1993. Accessed May 28, 2018. https://www.washingtonpost
.com/archive/lifestyle/1993/08/17/she-was-no-angel-thank-goodness
/a249995f-bc50-446f-a2f8-845f764a2c5e/?noredirect=on&utm_term
=.99bbd55dbb99.

Barker, Andrew. "Film Review: 'Wonder Woman.'" *Variety,* May 29, 2017. Accessed
August 26, 2018. https://variety.com/2017/film/reviews/film-review
-wonder-woman-1202446320/.

Barraclough, Leo. "Uma Thurman Explains How 'Kill Bill' Role Empowers Women."
Variety, July 2, 2017. Accessed August 1, 2018. https://variety.com/2017
/film/global/uma-thurman-kill-bill-quentin-tarantino-
women-1202486243/.

Breznican, Anthony. "Emma Watson on How Hermione Measures Up Beside Princess Leia." *Entertainment Weekly,* February 17, 2017. Accessed August 19,
2018. https://ew.com/movies/2017/02/17/emma-watson-how-hermione
-measures-up-beside-princess-leia/.

"Carrie Fisher Opens up About 'Star Wars', the Gold Bikini, and Her On-set Affair."
NPR.org, November 28, 2016. Accessed August 17, 2018. https://www.npr
.org/2016/11/28/503580112/carrie-fisher-opens-up-about-star-wars-the
-gold-bikini-and-her-on-set-affair.

Cwelich, Lorraine. "Callie Khouri's American Woman." *Interview,* February 6, 2014.
Accessed August 25, 2018. https://www.interviewmagazine.com/film
/callie-khouri-athena-film-festival.

Day, Elizabeth. "Geena Davis: After 'Thelma & Louise,' People Said Things Would
Improve for Women in Film. They Didn't." *The Guardian,* September 27,
2015. Accessed August 18, 2018. https://www.theguardian.com/film/2015
/sep/27/geena-davis-institute-sexism-in-film-industry.

Dockterman, Eliana. "Wonder Woman Breaks Through." *Time,* December 19, 2019.
Accessed August 26, 2018. http://time.com/4606107/wonder-woman
-breaks-through/.

Ebert, Roger. "Great Movie: 'The Color Purple.'" *Rogerebert.com,* March 28, 2004.
Accessed August 12, 2018. https://www.rogerebert.com/reviews/great
-movie-the-color-purple-1985.

———. "Whoopi Goldberg: 'The Color Purple.'" *Rogerebert.com,* December 15,
1985. Accessed August 12, 2018. https://www.rogerebert.com/interviews
/whoopi-goldberg-the-color-purple.

Freeman, Hadley. "James Cameron: 'The Downside of Being Attracted to Independent Women Is That They Don't Need You.'" *The Guardian*, August 24, 2017. Accessed June 3, 2018. https://www.theguardian.com/film/2017/aug/24/james-cameron-well-never-be-able-to-reproduce-the-shock-of-terminator-2.

Grow, Kory. "Silence of the Lambs at 25: It Broke All the Rules." *Rolling Stone*, February 12, 2016. Accessed July 31, 2018. https://www.rollingstone.com/movies/movie-news/silence-of-the-lambs-at-25-it-broke-all-the-rules-227905/.

Hayner, Chris E. "Inside Linda Hamilton's Insane Terminator 2 Training with James Cameron and Arnold Schwarzenegger." *Gamespot.com*, December 20, 2017. Accessed June 2, 2018. https://www.gamespot.com/articles/inside-linda-hamiltons-insane-terminator-2-trainin/1100-6455650/.

Hudson, Hannah Treweiler. "Q&A with *Hunger Games* Author Suzanne Collins." *Scholastic.com*, N.d. Accessed August 22, 2018. https://www.scholastic.com/teachers/articles/teaching-content/qa-hunger-games-author-suzanne-collins/.

"Ida Lupino." *DGA Quarterly*, Winter 2006. Accessed July 14, 2018. https://www.dga.org/Craft/DGAQ/All-Articles/0604-Winter2006-07/Legends-Ida-Lupino.aspx.

"Interview: Ang Lee on Crouching Tiger, Hidden Dragon." *Films in Review*, December 24, 2000. Accessed July 29, 2018. http://filmsinreview.com/2000/12/24/interview-ang-lee-crounching-tiger-hidden-dragon/ (site discontinued).

Israel, Robyn. "Not Just a Pretty Face: Erin Brockovich Proves the Power of One." *Palo Alto Online*, December 15, 2000. Accessed June 21, 2018. https://www.paloaltoonline.com/weekly/morgue/cover/2000_Dec_15.ERINBROK.html.

"Joan Fontaine, Oscar-winning Actress, Dies at 96." *The Guardian*, December 15, 2013. Accessed August 3, 2018. https://www.theguardian.com/film/2013/dec/16/joan-fontaine-oscar-winning-actor-dies-at-96.

Konow, David. "Dan O'Bannon and the Origins of 'Alien.'" *Tested*, November 4, 2013. Accessed August 7, 2018. https://www.tested.com/art/movies/458897-dan-obannon-and-origins-alien/.

Li, Shirley. "Sigourney Weaver Says Sci-fi 'Reflects How Powerful Women Are.'" *Entertainment Weekly*, July 17, 2017. Accessed August 7, 2018. https://ew.com/movies/2017/07/17/sigourney-weaver-sci-fi-roles-women-power/.

McCarthy, Kelly. "Angela Bassett Brings 'A Little of That Essence' as Tina Turner to

Inspire Other Female Leads." *ABC News,* July 23, 2018. Accessed August 12, 2018. https://abcnews.go.com/GMA/Culture/angela-bassett-brings -essence-tina-turner-inspire-female/story?id=56754250.

Setoodeh, Ramin. "Wonder Woman Director Patty Jenkins on Equal Pay, Hollywood Sexism, and James Cameron's Nasty Words." *Variety,* October 10, 2017. Accessed August 26, 2018. https://variety.com/2017/film/features /patty-jenkins-wonder-woman-hollywood-sexism-equal-pay-james -cameron-1202583237/.

Vallance, Tom. "Obituary: Catherine Turney." *The Independent,* September 16, 1998. Accessed July 1, 2018. https://www.independent.co.uk/arts -entertainment/obituary-catherine-turney-1198417.html.

Watson, Emma. "Emma's Interview with J.K. Rowling." *EmmaWatson.com,* February/March 2014. Accessed August 19, 2018. http://emma-watson .net/2014/02/07/emmas-interview-with-jk-rowling/.

Zemler, Emily. "Has Mad Max Given Us a Truly Feminist Action Star? Charlize Theron Thinks So." *Elle.com,* May 24, 2015. Accessed August 25, 2018. https://www.elle.com/culture/movies-tv/a28156/charlize -theron-mad-max-interview/.

Audio/Video

Berry, Halle. "Halle Berry Wins Best Actress TV Movie—Golden Globes 2000." YouTube video, 3:14, posted by "AwardsShowNetwork," October 25, 2010. https://www.youtube.com/watch?v=6xNp37oWEiM.

Biography. "Ida Lupino: Through the Lens." Produced by Torrie Rozenzweig. Written by Gidion Phillips. A&E Networks, March 24, 1998.

Bowman, Edith. "In Conversation with . . . Jodie Foster, on The Silence of the Lambs." YouTube video, 36:57, posted by "BFI," November 16, 2017. https://www.youtube.com/watch?v=ZETEx_uAq9g.

Colbert, Stephen. "Carrie Fisher: Even in Space, There's a Double Standard for Women." YouTube video, 6:58, posted by "The Late Show with Stephen Colbert," November 22, 2016. https://www.youtube.com/watch?v= R1E6IexeSrQ.

Hayek, Salma. "A Conversation with Salma Hayek." Disc 1. *Frida,* special edition DVD. Directed by Julie Taymor. Santa Monica, CA: Miramax Home Enter- tainment, 2003.

Hill, Jack. "Commentary." *Coffy*, DVD. Directed by Jack Hill. Santa Monica, CA: MGM Home Entertainment, 2001.

"Kate Winslet on Mildred Pierce (Venice Film Festival)." YouTube video, 7:05, posted by "ETV Film, Inc.," September 3, 2011. https://www.youtube.com /watch?v=7GJhWXd3X3E.

"Katharine Hepburn—Documentary." YouTube video, 43:53, posted by "Film Historian," September 22, 2016. https://www.youtube.com/watch?v= 5A4KYLu3fQA.

Lucas, George. "Empire of Dreams." Disc 4. *Star Wars* Trilogy Box Set, DVD. Directed by Kevin Burns. Beverly Hills, CA: Twentieth Century Fox Home Entertainment, 2004.

Pollack, Sydney. "Feature Commentary." Disc 1. *Out of Africa*, special 100th anniversary collector's edition DVD. Directed by Sydney Pollack. Universal City, CA.: Universal Home Entertainment, 2012.

Rose, Charlie. "Julia Roberts." Charlie Rose video, 54:06. March 14, 2000. https:// charlierose.com/videos/23349.

Scott, Ridley. "Audio Commentaries." *Thelma & Louise*, DVD. Directed by Ridley Scott. Santa Monica, CA: MGM Home Entertainment, 2004.

Streep, Meryl. "A Song of Africa." Disc 2. *Out of Africa*, special 100th anniversary collector's edition DVD. Directed by Sydney Pollack. Universal City, Calif.: Universal Home Entertainment, 2012.

Taymor, Julie. "Feature Commentary." Disc 1. *Frida*, special edition DVD. Directed by Julie Taymor. Santa Monica, CA: Miramax Home Entertainment, 2003.

"The Hunger Games: Jennifer Lawrence Interview—2012." YouTube video, 6:35, posted by "Movieclips Coming Soon," March 12, 2012. https://www .youtube.com/watch?v=82jYp0TU0XY.

"The Hunger Games: Jennifer Lawrence Interview on Katniss Everdeen." YouTube video, 0:27, posted by "TheCelebFactory," April 4, 2012. https://www .youtube.com/watch?v=RHfIR0ZGV1A.

Vance, Jeffrey, and Tony Maietta. "Commentary." *The Divorcee*, TCM Archives: Forbidden Hollywood Collection Vol. II DVD. Directed by Robert Z. Leonard. Burbank, CA: Warner Home Video, 2006.

Other Materials

Wagner, Natasha Gregson. Conversation with the author, January 11, 2018.

Westall, Susan. "Ursula Parrott: A Bio-Bibliography." Master's thesis, Kent State University, July 1999. https://files.eric.ed.gov/fulltext/ED435388.pdf.

Websites

https://catalog.afi.com/

www.agathachristie.com

www.imdb.com

www.lapl.org

www.starwars.com

www.tcm.com

www.wikipedia.org

Photo Credits

All images in this book are from Independent Visions Archive, the Turner Classic Movies Archive, and the author's collection, with the exceptions of:

Pages xiii, 20, 21, 24, 25, 88, 204, and 207 courtesy Bison Archives

Pages 44, 46, 47, 108, and 126 courtesy Matt Tunia Collection

Pages 32 and 35 courtesy David Wills Collection

Images from the Independent Visions Archive are exclusively represented by mptv. For more information regarding licensing or purchasing images from mptv, please contact mptvimages at www.mptvimages.com.

The photos and images in this book are for educational purposes, and while every effort has been made to identify the proper photographer and/or copyright holders, some photos had no accreditation. In these cases, if proper credit and/or copyright is discovered, credits will be added in subsequent printings.

A wardrobe test for Joan Crawford in *Mildred Pierce*

Index

Acknowledgments

Heartfelt thanks to everyone who helped me navigate the challenges I encountered in bringing this book to life.

Eternal gratitude to my editor, Cindy De La Hoz, who not only suggested the entire concept, but also encouraged my ideas, respected my opinions, and championed my choices, even when the going got rough. Cindy, I hope this book is everything you envisioned.

Endless thanks to Manoah Bowman for his unwavering belief in my talent, for his creative input, and for generously allowing access to his amazing images.

For contributing a fabulous foreword under a last-minute time crunch, a million thanks to superheroine Julie Newmar.

I would also like to thank Matt Tunia, Marc Wanamaker, David Wills, Luisa Ribeiro, Emily Carman, Karie Bible, Natasha Gregson Wagner, and Robert Wagner for their kindness and assistance. Thanks to my mom and my family and friends in Texas for their long-distance support and to Camilla Jackson for her help in brainstorming the perfect title.

I am truly grateful to everyone at the female-driven Running Press (guys too!), including Amanda Richmond, Katie Hubbard, Kristin Kiser, Jennifer Kasius, and Seta Zink. Special thanks to Michael Clark and April Rondeau for carrying this book through the final stages of the editorial process.

Many thanks to the Turner Classic Movies staff, especially John Malahy, Heather Margolis, Pola Chagnon, Genevieve McGillicuddy, and Jennifer Dorian. Thanks to Aaron Spiegeland at Parham Santana.

A special shout-out to the Margaret Herrick Library and the Los Angeles Public Library System. Long live the libraries of America.